DEEP FIELD

ABOUT THE AUTHOR

Tom Bamforth is an Australian aid worker whose writing has appeared in *The Age*, *Granta* and *Griffith Review*. He experienced the 2005 Pakistan earthquake first hand while on an archaeological tour and has subsequently worked in natural disaster and conflict areas in Pakistan's North West Frontier Province and Kashmir, Sudan's Darfur states, the Philippines' Mindanao region and across the Pacific Islands.

An SBS Book

Published in 2014 by Hardie Grant Books

Hardie Grant Books (Australia)
Ground Floor, Building 1
658 Church Street
Richmond, Victoria 3121
www.hardiegrant.com.au

Hardie Grant Books (UK)
Dudley House, North Suite
34–35 Southampton Street
London WC2E 7HF
www.hardiegrant.co.uk

Cataloguing in publication data is available from the National Library of Australia
Deep Field
ISBN 9 781742703800

Design by Peter Daniel
Cover image courtesy of Getty Images
CIA World Factbook Political World Map courtesy Wikimedia Commons
Typeset in ITC New Baskerville 11/17pt
Printed and bound in Australia by Griffin Press

DEEP FIELD

DISPATCHES FROM THE FRONTLINES OF AID RELIEF
FROM PAKISTAN TO KAZAN, THE PUNJAB TO THE PACIFIC

TOM BAMFORTH

hardie grant books
MELBOURNE · LONDON

CONTENTS

PREFACE
MAE HONG SON REFUGEE CAMP, THAILAND

Children ran through the streets, men played volleyball on the central *maidan*, and the sounds of music, laughter and learning drifted from the schools on the humid afternoon air. The cool houses with deep eaves and thatched roofs were a far cry from the squalid settlements where I had worked with other refugees fleeing war and natural disaster. In Pakistan families froze in the rain and mud of the Himalayan winter, living for months beside open sewers and in ancient canvas tents. In Sudan vast temporary cities grew in the desert. They were violent microcosms of conflict, unemployment and persecution. Women risked attack in the daily search for water and firewood. I had braced myself before arriving at the Mae Hong Son refugee camp, on the Thai–Burma border, but I found myself in a pleasant village of ethnic Karennyi refugees.

Resplendent in a pink shirt and fresh from a recent scholarship to Oxford, the Thai camp commander dazzled with his enamelled self-confidence, his progressive views and his conviction that he was soaring to the top. Here were schools and resources, committed NGOs. The Commander expressed his concern for the plight of the refugees, and declared his willingness to bend the strict application of Thai law in order to allow the people in the camp the chance to lead lives that were as ordinary as possible. His body language acted out his words of friendship and unity —a supportive hand on the shoulder, a touch of the arm, a courteous incline of the head.

But this was more like 19th-century Russia than the modern day: a liberal feudal—almost falsely at ease— presented his progressive 'new model' village. For him, this was a harmonious, almost Tolstoyan, experiment where 16,000 people would lead the ordinary lives that had been denied them by their own state, under the watchful beneficent patriarch of Thailand. There was even a decent enough clinic, staffed and equipped, and roosters mean-dered in and out of the maternity ward. Once the women in the community knew I was coming, endless streams of woven shawls and fabrics were produced for sale. The air of the place appeared to be one of functionality, normality, even jollity.

The reality of refugee life in Thailand, however, takes place below the choreographed surface of such interac-tions. Subtle hints of a different world would occasionally emerge through the cloud of bonhomie and busy, but ulti-mately purposeless, activity.

Men in uniform accompanied me everywhere and took an endless series of photos—some of which found their way onto the Commander's Facebook page. And when the Commander placed an empathetic and comradely arm

around the refugees to whom I spoke, they recoiled percep-
tibly. Even if he was one of the more liberal bureaucrats,
with populist sympathies, he was still a representative of
a state that had not signed the UNHCR Refugee Convention. It is also a state that has created an elaborate system
of variegated citizenship and residency rights that excludes
as many as three million people (refugees and hill tribes)
from its formal legal protection, keeping them in a condition of economic and social vulnerability. To benefit from
this influx of stateless people, the Thai government had
established major manufacturing centres along the border
where labour is cheap and desperate and rights are few.
Human traffickers lurk near here, promising better futures
for the rural poor, who instead are led into a sexual and
industrial slavery that would be unimaginable were it not
real.

The impression of ordinary village life was similarly
misleading—refugees could not legally leave the camp,
could not work or gain access to the upper levels of the
Thai education system. While rules were periodically bent,
the refugees were entirely reliant on the ongoing delivery
of food and supplies by aid agencies and had lived in this
condition of compound, inter-generational dependency
for twenty-five years. With the financial crisis, aid budgets
had been cut and already food supplies had been reduced.
Discussions about sustainability and potential camp closure
had begun.

The Karennyi refugees could not return home while the
Burmese state continued its persecution of ethnic minorities. Mistaking the friendliness of the camp commander for
genuine openness, I asked about the political affiliations

of the refugees. Did they have contact with opposition groups in exile in Thailand? Under what conditions would they return to Burma? But silence descended on the group when I asked the commander to discuss anything beyond the realities of daily life in the camp and the perennial wait for return or resettlement. The collapse of minority opposition to the Burmese state in the mid-nineties and regular military action since then had left behind a deeply damaged homeland under military occupation. Those who remained faced the brutalising force of an occupying regime: forced labour, land confiscation, involuntary relocation, arbitrary (in)justice including detainment and execution, sexual violence and environmental degradation left by government-controlled mining and forestry interests. Resettlement of the entire community had been offered by Scandinavian, Australian and US governments, but few—especially the older refugees—were willing to resettle and risk losing their identity, their culture and the possibility, however remote, of going home. What, after a life of farming in the Burmese hills, would such people do in freezing Minnesota, where most were granted resettlement? Effectively, the majority were stuck in an intergenerational limbo that would not end until the fall of the current Burmese regime or the Thai government lost its patience.

While some of the refugees joined opposition militias and tried to fight on, others were resigned, their slowly fading hope forming corrosive lines across their faces. Some, like a young schoolteacher, tried to impart language and computer skills to those seeking a future overseas. A local self-help group, the Karennyi National

Women's Organisation, combined fiery political activism with household industry to generate at least some income. It was the women who carried on, kept things together and were politically active; their high seriousness and dedication were astounding. They were the economic foundation of the refugee community's survival, starting cottage industries and continuing traditional crafts, selling hand-woven clothes to the tourists who flocked to northern Thailand. When I met them at a fabric-making workshop outside the camp, I found that they were direct and politically assertive in the way that the men were not. They were proud members of the Karennyi National Women's Organisation, dedicated both to improving the economic and social conditions of refugee Karennyi women as well as the broader political goal of returning home to a fully democratic Burma.

A malaise seemed to have descended over the men. Some younger ones had returned to the jungles to fight with Karennyi militia against government occupation of their ethnic homelands. They had quickly realised, however, the futility of taking on the well-supplied Burmese army and had become disillusioned by the fractured politics of the hill-tribe opposition movements, which had been militarily defeated more than fifteen years before. So not for these refugees the exuberance and hugs of the camp commander. Theirs was a limbo for which a workable solution would not be found within their lifetimes.

Those who were able to leave did so with nothing, their future sealed in an envelope containing a chest X-ray and bearing the random letters that would shape the rest of their lives—an identification number and the formula:

MHS/IOM/MIN (Mae Hong Song Camp–International Organisation for Migration–Minnesota). For the remaining three million who had fled war and persecution across the border, not even this was an option.

Today, there are 1.3 billion people living on less than a dollar a day (350 million of whom are children). Globally, there are approximately 42 million refugees, as well as 27 million internally displaced people who can no longer live in their homes but remain within their own countries. Humanitarian work alone cannot provide safe lives and livelihoods for people affected by poverty, conflict, drought, famine and war—and neither, it would appear, can our national and international political institutions that are so narrowly established to promote their own, often bizarre, assessments of monetary and military self-interest. The world is consequently in dire need of humanitarians—the overwhelming majority of whom are not 'aid workers' as such but the immediate friends, family, colleagues and social networks of people affected by disasters and conflict.

Still more important, however, is the reclamation of political ground by global citizens who perhaps one day can take human rights back from lawyers with their accountancy of rules, take livelihoods away from the tinkering of economists, and restore power to parliaments rather than generals, corporations and the military-industrial complex. Humanitarianism is perhaps a beginning, even an idea. In the words of one aid worker: it is 'an attempt to bring a measure of humanity, always insufficient, into situations that should not exist'. Not enough, clearly, but at least it is a start and an attempt to engage with the world's events with the human virtues of compassion and consideration rather than the calculus of mercantile self-interest that is the cause of so much of today's inequality.

But I had not started out intending to work in the humanitarian world. For most, despite the increasing number of courses and certificates for would-be aid workers, the path to this kind of work is as tangential as the places where disasters and conflicts occur. It was an earthquake in Pakistan while I was on holiday exploring the mountains and monuments of the country's north that propelled me suddenly and unexpectedly into the maelstrom of my first response.

PART 1
PAKISTAN, 2005

COLONELS, CRICKET AND WINTER IN THE HIMALAYAS

CHAPTER 1
THE ELUSIVE MR SCOTCH

THE NUMBERS ROSE SLOWLY, like a cricket innings, and the commentators droned. There was little new information and the television news recycled the same pictures, overlaid with a boxed scorecard showing a slowly growing body count. An apartment complex in Islamabad had collapsed: fifteen people missing. An hour later it had turned to twenty-five; by mid-afternoon it was 150. The army had been called up, and stood around with guns looking helpless as rapid-reaction teams with sniffer dogs arrived to pull the living from the vast pile of concrete and dust. With every news update, the death toll rose steadily and threatened to continue.

For me, living in Pakistan's North West Frontier Province[1] in 2005, this was no distant event. I had felt the ground shake violently, and took cover under my bed as plaster fell

---

[1] Now known as Khyber-Pakhtunkhwa (KPK) in deference to Pashtun ethno-nationalist aspirations.

from the ceiling and furniture crashed around me. For a moment the walls and the ceiling had seemed to sway in a disjointed waltz. I watched as the fan slowly detached itself from the ceiling, and calculated that it was too late to bolt down three flights of stairs. I had heard the term 'triangulation'—getting down next to a solid object so that when the roof came down it would form a small, triangular, survivable space. But the furniture didn't look that solid. As I got down next to the bed, the earth moved again—first from side to side, and then up and down in jolts.

And in those minutes, shortly before breakfast on a Saturday morning, 83,000 people were crushed to death. A further three million were instantly rendered homeless across the hills of the Karakorum and the Himalaya.

I knew nothing of this at the time. After the hotel stopped shaking I went out into the bustling town of Mingora, in the Swat Valley (later the site of a major battle against the Pakistani Taliban), and continued what I had left Australia to do: explore the astonishing ancient remains of Indo-Hellenic civilisation which had spread across Pakistan's northern plains and into the foothills of the Hindu Kush. Oblivious to the news of the earthquake slowly trickling in, I climbed amid the ruined monasteries and universities of the Bactrian Greeks, whose mesmeric fusion of Greek and Buddhist cultures scatters the Gandhara Plains from Kabul to Peshawar and the outskirts of Islamabad. I pored over ancient coins embossed with the profile of Alexander the Great, and sculptures of curly-haired, toga-clad Buddhas.[2] My Muslim guides spoke of the importance of pluralism,

---

[2] In Pakistan today, the remote Kalash Valley is inhabited by an animist tribe of fair-skinned, light-eyed people who drink wine from amphorae and who are said to be the descendants of Alexander's armies.

the subjectivity of truth and the arcane theological meaning embodied in the myriad poses of Greco-Buddhist statues exquisitely preserved in the stone of the North West Frontier.

One guide had studied to be a teacher in Russia and returned to the Swat Valley because of its strong educational traditions. He used to take his classes around the ruins, explaining to them the pre-Islamic history of the region. When I got back to the hotel that evening I received a call from ABC Radio National, desperately seeking an Australian 'eyewitness' to the earthquake. 'Is there a danger,' the interviewer asked, 'that orphans will attend madrasahs and become the next generation of terrorists?'

While the cosmic stone masonry of the Bactrian Greeks had lasted the millennia, the squat concrete structures of modern Pakistan disintegrated in seconds. Back in Islamabad some days later, I could see the true scale of the catastrophe. I attended public meetings of the UN coordination team, and the situation looked desperate. The earthquake had ripped across the entire north of the country, shattering cities and destroying villages. There were insufficient resources, mountain roads had been swept away and thousands of small villages at vast altitudes were inaccessible. Helicopters had been ordered to fly reconnaissance and aid sorties over the deep valleys of Pakistan's north—but there were too few of these available. Most of the army's 114 Chinooks were engaged fighting a nebulous 'war on terror' in the country's tribal agencies and could not be recalled. In any case, we were told, it was technically too difficult to remove the machine-gun awnings to make way for cargoes of aid.

For forty-eight hours the international media circus descended on the city—flown in from New York, London, Paris, Brussels and Tehran—to capture on camera the reeling of a concussed nation and the growing stench of its stricken cities, before flying out again. Night after night the TV news brought updates and crossed live to journalists in Islamabad solemnly intoning the 'universal truths' about Pakistan: a nuclear-armed Islamic state beset by 'terror, the bomb and military rule'.

I recalled the words of my Russian history lecturer from university, who had said he wanted to rescue the past, and consequently the present, from theorists and commentators who saw the world in terms of systems rather than societies. In Pakistan the same experts and analysts had migrated from Soviet studies to the more fashionable concerns of terrorism, Islam and South Asia. Having failed to predict the demise of the Soviet Union in their previous careers, they were now equally unable to account for Pakistan's resilience. But for the surviving three million people in the distant hills of the Himalayas, brutally dislodged from their mountain fastness, facing rain and sleet and snow and ice, these debates were meaningless.

Amid the chaos of the early response, I volunteered at a local charity and spent an afternoon loading trucks with anything people could throw together to send into the mountains. Blankets, jumpers, bedding and food arrived from across the country, the donors all knowing there would be little hope for the millions of earthquake survivors once the Himalayan winter set in. I sat in a small circle with the charity's founder—a Gandhian figure whose humility, simplicity and

perhaps feigned illiteracy were a foil for his immense organ-
isational abilities and intellect. He had founded the country's
only national ambulance service, and a network of schools
and orphanages. Deeply devout, he was asked by one woman
seeking to imitate the depths of his Islamic belief how many
times he prayed each day. 'Sister,' he replied with more than
a hint of the Mahatma's wit, 'I deal in wholesale, not retail.'

Wanting to do more than load trucks, I was tipped off by a
friend that an international aid organisation was expanding
its operations and needed people for more substantive work.
I was invited to an interview with the operations manager,
who already looked haggard and overworked. We sat on
director's chairs in a garden in a leafy and subdued Islamabad suburb. He looked over my CV for a few minutes before
asking if I liked camping. 'Very much,' I lied, and tried to
look as if I meant it while he examined me for an unnerving
moment before throwing his hands up in resignation. 'Look,
you can walk, you can talk and right now we need bodies on
the ground. Do you know where I can get a case of Scotch in
Islamabad?' Fortuitously, I had just been given the number
of shady local alcohol supplier known simply as Mr Scotch.
I was hired.

The following day I was put in a car and driven to Mansehra,
the town that would become a hub for the relief effort in
the North West Frontier Province and my home for the next
eighteen months. I had no idea what I would be doing or
who I would be working with. The first signs weren't good.

I was offered a job helping to coordinate all aid agencies
working to provide emergency shelter across the North West
Frontier Province—a job that was for me a vertical learning
curve and had to be performed under acute pressure. For

weeks during the early stages of the response, I slept next to my desk in a makeshift office and still wished I could spend more time working. 'Don't worry,' one faintly sympathetic colleague assured me, 'as a coordinator, you have all the responsibility for an effective response and none of the power to ensure this happens.'

'We're basically a humane trucking company,' my new employer told me when I reported for my first day of work. I'd had the temerity to ask what the organisation and, by extension, I would be doing. 'We started sending people home after World War Two and are basically doing the same thing today. Although,' he added reflectively, 'much of what we now do is to try to get people to stay where they are—it's much easier for us all that way.' It was a pragmatic introduction to humanitarian work and largely devoid of ideology or ethical position. In a 'yee-ha' moment sometime later I saw him high-five another new colleague with the words 'Savin' lives—makes you feel damn good, don't it?' as he got back into a car after dropping me at my new office—a collapsed primary school in Pakistan's North West Frontier Province. 'Imbecile,' someone muttered as the car took off, away from the place where lives might be saved and back to the capital, Islamabad. Unlike headquarters, field offices are often unsentimental places.

In some ways, however, this description of my new aid agency's work was refreshing in its bluntness and enthusiasm, even if it did reveal a paradox of humanitarian work. Much of the rise in international funding was motivated not by compassion but by fear—keeping people at home would potentially limit the number of refugees and asylum-seekers making their way to wealthier countries in an increasingly immigrant-phobic world. In this view, addressing the consequences as well as the 'root causes' of crises through humanitarian work and longer-term development programs would reduce insecurity and instability while promoting what has increasingly come to be known as 'human security'. Ultimately, it was hoped, development programs and effective humanitarian response would prevent 'state failure' and forced migration to the borders of Western Europe, the US and Australia. For many donors, humanitarian response was as much a moral imperative as it was a product of perceived military, economic and political necessity. It nicely linked altruistic ambitions and self-interested concerns—terrorism, migration, domestic voter reactions. It has led to what commentators have called the 'securitisation of aid', promoting not only security in countries affected by turbulence and turmoil but also security from perceived external threats within the donor states themselves. The terrorists who had attacked the Twin Towers in New York and their al-Qaeda controllers took refuge in such 'failed' or 'failing' states—Afghanistan, Pakistan, Sudan and Somalia. Aid programs were seen as a way to provide an alternative to the political manifestations of extremism in countries suffering state breakdown, war and poverty. 'Keeping people at home' through humanitarian action was, therefore, in part a strategic response to Western security concerns.

The institution I worked for—International Organization for Migration (IOM)—saw itself as offering a pragmatic, practical service unburdened by ideology or even a desire to make the world in some way a better place. IOM was not an NGO, nor was it quite a member of the UN 'family', although it did take on a number of UN functions, and its employees travelled around in cars labelled with the familiar blue lettering and flags of the UN. Yet its independence from the UN system and its lack of clear humanitarian founding principles or mandates meant that it frequently provoked animosity among its more established half-siblings—an animosity that combined institutional rivalry and occasional personal hostility with ethical concerns about what a 'proper' NGO or UN agency was actually about.

'Do you realise,' I was asked as I innocently walked into one of my first aid coordination meetings with the heads of various UN agencies, 'that you are working for the bastard child of the UN?' Unacknowledged and often mistrusted, IOM frequently undertook work that was controversial, not strictly humanitarian, and ultimately informed by the combined development and security preoccupations of the UN member states that funded it.

Far from the aspirations of headquarters, students and people at home, the field offices were absorbed in the mire of daily activity—its chaos and challenges—and this left little room for overt expressions of idealism. We were 'international civil servants' and did what we were funded to do. In part this was because of vague ideas about being 'humane' to people who were forced to move as a consequence of war or natural disaster. It was also because the organisation was 'paratatal', as the phrase went—effectively a private arm of government—and could be subcontracted to do difficult work in difficult places that was in some vague way related to population movements. This was work that ranged from emergency response to managing elections in Iraq and Afghanistan—programs that were funded by the very countries whose troops made up the NATO forces, Britain and the US. It was an agency to which the business of government could be farmed out to provide the cover of independence and plausibility. In Pakistan, the organisation's interest in migration (and anything linked to it—which was basically everything the aid world had to offer) had led it to play a leading role in the coordination of emergency response, for which it had no pre-existing mandate or expertise.

The first humanitarians have always been the family, friends, neighbours and community associations of those immediately affected by disasters: the people themselves. The state and its resources—civil defence and military organisations—have been a problematic and sometimes slow second, and in some cases state action or inaction exacerbates the disaster itself. A distant third in the race to assist has tended to be what is perhaps misleading called the 'international community'—a phrase that evokes a homely sense of common purpose that is completely lacking in either the political mechanisms for international decision-making—such as the UN Security Council or the General Assembly, or the international mechanisms for humanitarian response. To echo the phrase of fictitious British bureaucrat Sir Humphrey Appleby, the organisations that manage a humanitarian response are less a caring community of practitioners and donors than something more reminiscent of a confederacy of warring tribes each with its own agenda, 'mandate', source of funding and, increasingly, sense of self-proclaimed moral purpose.

The humanitarian sector is now rapidly developing into a profession. It is estimated that there are more than 200,000 aid workers active around the globe, as well as an uncountable number of international NGOs and organisations devoted to aid and development assistance, sometimes estimated at about 40,000 organisations that operate internationally, in one way or another. This level of interest and engagement is a far cry from the 'early days' before communications technology when, as a colleague once told me, he was sent a letter by the British Red Cross which said it thought 'there may be something happening in Uganda' and was given $20,000 in cash and a motorbike and told to 'do something about it'. Despite being a rapidly professionalising, multi-billion-dollar 'industry', humanitarian work—given that it takes place in crisis situations—is still often ad hoc, driven by people rather than systems and, above all, accidental.

While I was completely new to the practice of humanitarian response—the roles, mandates and responsibilities of different aid agencies, and especially to the specialised role of aid coordination—I was not entirely lost. I had some understanding, by the time the earthquake hit, about the Pakistan context. I had studied its history and politics and, bizarrely, because of a youthful phase reading widely in Russian literature, I somehow felt that working in an emergency response was strangely familiar. It was far from the smooth bureaucratic operation I had imagined, with clear roles and leaders and the rest of us following along in well-marked footsteps. Instead, the response was very much the embodiment, in crisis, of the institutions, interests, and personal and political ideological conflicts with which Pakistan was obsessed and which fill the moving, funny and periodically tortured pages of the best Russian novels. Understanding this 'personality-driven' context was as important as knowing about the guiding principles and best practices of humanitarian assistance. Each night, I climbed into my sleeping bag with two books: the sections of the various humanitarian guides that I felt I needed to learn about and a copy of Tolstoy's *Anna Karenina*. In the end, it was probably *Anna Karenina* that provided the better guide, with its intensely complex and fractious set of embedded social relationships that reflected the way that disasters and conflicts, too, are social phenomena. Tolstoy famously begins the book with the statement that 'all happy families are alike; each unhappy family is unhappy in its own way'—something that could easily describe the collective achievements and failures of people and institutions responding to crises: a collective enterprise of liberal internationalist values that, with its humanity and its flaws, never quite lives up to the 'happy family' ideal.

I was dropped off at a small collapsed primary school, which was where I slept and where our makeshift headquarters would be situated for the next few weeks. Ostensibly we were coordinating all organisations providing emergency shelter to the more than 700,000 people who had lost their homes during the earthquake. We had been lent some space amid the concrete debris by a mobile German medical unit that had quartered there, and during the day we set up our office on a series of string beds, one of which we turned on its head and moved every half-hour following the sun, to provide shade. Every few minutes the dull thud of rotor blades roared overhead as NATO helicopters—sent over from Afghanistan—flew past on aid missions. The nights were bitterly cold, and even though I slept in a cracked classroom I learned quickly to leave my sleeping bag open and to run out into the courtyard every time there was an aftershock—which came frequently and massively in the aftermath of that first tectonic jolt.

IOM had been given a central role in the relief effort but had taken some time to scale up its operations to respond on the massive scale required. When we arrived, our reception was harsh. We were addressed by our institutional acronym, rather than by name. The multi-pocketed, pseudo-military jerkins we wore quickly became known as 'the target', owing to the organisation's round logo and the hostile response it guaranteed. As they subsequently became an established part of 'field wear', sported by anyone who wished to suggest they had somehow been 'at the front', they became known as 'the wanker jacket'. 'Don't you realise there's been an earthquake?' I was asked early on by one exasperated aid worker who, ironically, had come to us for help.

The nights were equally unremitting, and what was officially termed 'the close of play' began sometime after 10pm with the announcement of an hour of reflection—a sort of humanitarian Nunc Dimittis, complete with the swirling smoke of Raj-nostalgic cigarettes: Player's, Pall Mall, Craven A. We called this almost religious moment 'fuck-up of the day'.

But information on the earthquake was limited and uncoordinated. Reports dribbled in from field staff of new population movements, uncontacted villages and whole districts in the mountains still reeling from aftershocks. Random shell-shocked people would turn up at our door asking for aid, sometimes with battered handwritten letters of supplication in English or Urdu that had clearly been taken from aid agency to aid agency in the hope of finding a tent, sleeping bag or box of military rations.

I spent a day with a team conducting aerial assessments of the northern valleys most severely hit by the earthquake. I had read the reports and seen some footage but only after eight hours in a helicopter, weaving in and out of the valleys, did I begin to comprehend the full picture. From on high little damage could be seen, but as we swooped low on unsuspecting hamlets clustered together at altitudes of up to 10,000 feet, the destructive power that had been unleashed across these vast alpine tracts was awesome. Roofs of houses that looked intact from above were suddenly revealed to be unsupported by walls and sat a few feet off the ground, covering the debris that had crushed those inside. Roads, carved through the vast mountains over decades with conscripted muscle and dynamite, had been swept away in seconds, cutting off whole regions from the outside world. In a land of swallowed roads and shattered bridges, everything covered in a grey dust of concrete, rubble and brick, only the domed mosques—built, ironically, for another world—continued to stand.

In a few places we landed, blowing down tents and covering the landscape and its inhabitants with dust from the helicopter's downdraft. We leapt out clutching notebooks and GPS units, vigorously recording our altitude, coordinates and observations, as if this rush of note-taking would somehow shrink mountains, unify villages and bring order to chaos.

But this new appreciation for the enormity of the disaster only diminished our feeble initial response. After some days trying to establish a presence in Mansehra and acting as the de facto punching bag for the international community, I was sent north to the town of Balakot to assess the effectiveness of our operations there. I had never seen a disaster zone like this before: the scene was shocking and unreal, familiar to me only from the grainy footage of post-apocalyptic Hiroshima after the flight of the *Enola Gay*. Towering snow-capped peaks were etched sharply against the sky like monumental tombstones, standing guard over the remains of a city of 30,000 people now compacted to little more than knee height. No structures remained standing. Even in the ruins of the town the air was so clear it crackled with each breath and the vertiginous scale of the mountains lent a paradoxical clarity and euphoria to a scene of confusion, disorientation and loss. Men and women walked through the former streets at once familiar and yet now vanished, displaced strangers amid the destruction of their own home.

Strangely, given northern Pakistan's conservative patriarchal society, I saw a young girl leading her father, bleeding from the head and evidently unable to see, towards a Pakistan Red Crescent field hospital. As if responding to the absurdity of a world turned upside down, fruit sellers had set up stalls in the rubble of a collapsed market, offering their oranges to non-existent crowds. A green-domed mosque—the sole surviving building—emitted a call to prayer, a lone human voice that echoed hauntingly in the brutal grandeur of the valley.

Our set-up in Balakot was dysfunctional and needed almost as much assistance as the homeless former residents themselves. Huddling in leaky canvas tents, wallowing in sludge, already coughing from bronchial infections and ineffectually led, our team of Pashtuns was demoralised and at breaking point. I had been sent up in an effort to take control of the local operation and get evidence to dismiss its venal and incompetent international manager—Jabba the

Hutt, as he had become known. On arrival I had received a message from headquarters in Islamabad to 'rock no boats', and I had no authority to intervene in the operation or the treatment of staff. 'I will eat him,' roared one of my Pashtun colleagues in rage, having just been dismissed for the unpardonable crime of being competent. It was a mess: the city was destroyed, our operational response was useless, and its field management beyond redemption. As I walked out of yet another freezing tent I stumbled into a muddy and treacherous area by the riverbank that turned out to be an open sewer. Everything in that place on that day seemed cursed.

Back in Islamabad I met with our new operations manager, an American with pale blue eyes and slightly bucked front teeth whose number was listed in my phone as Bugs. New to the business of aid and overwhelmed by the enormousness of the task ahead of us, I hoped he would give me some clear direction and advice. We discussed the weather and his recent visit to Indonesia, and before heading off he handed me a brown envelope. 'Read this on your way back,' he said. 'It'll give a you a good idea of what we're all about.' In the car I tore open the envelope, looking for the instructions that would solve the earthquake and provide winter shelters for the almost one million people who were now homeless. 'Proposal for Rubble Removal,' the document said. Back at base—amid the debris of the former primary school—my emails addressed to 'Rubble Rouser' and 'Rubble with a Cause' went unanswered.

CHAPTER 2
SOCIAL ABBOTTABAD AND THE FRONTIER FORCE OFFICERS' MESS

'YOU KNOW, TOM,' said Colonel Mohsin, 'I was once a POW.' The colonel was in an expansive postprandial mood as we settled on the verandah of the Frontier Force Officers' Mess in the leafy garrison town of Abbottabad.

I had known Col. Mohsin (Retd) for some time now. He had appeared one day at our office with a brilliantly trimmed moustache, regimental cravat, and cuffs that crackled and shot with every opportunity. Since then he had managed a vast logistics operation—300 trucks, drivers and field staff—moving hundreds of thousands of tarpaulins, blankets, mattresses, tents, tools, clothes, and tens of thousands of people around the treacherous mountain roads with sangfroid and studied understatement. He had converted our office into an operation and had, with his years in the army, brought the art of war into the business of aid. Because of him, there was purpose in our work and the rooms were now covered in maps, diagrams and checklists; the atmosphere was a strangely relaxed, avuncular authority. Everyone now addressed each other as *bhai* (brother) or *bhaji* (sister), while heels clicked and salutes were given in the corridors of what had become a humanitarian war room.

Behind the nicotine-fuelled histrionics of the internationals, so visible during the initial phases of the earthquake response, our Pakistani friends and colleagues had brought order, humour, clarity, dignity and direction to the response. 'Thank God the earthquake happened here,' one departing aid worker told me. 'We would have been lost anywhere else.' With Colonel Mohsin and my indomitable colleagues—Shahab, Zubair, Usman and Samira—grinning broadly in response to each new setback (and there were many), we thought we could do anything. One glorious day I overheard Shahab, a fearlessly self-confident Pashtun, talking to a recently arrived international head of a major UN agency. 'Boy,' he commanded across the gulf of rank and pay, 'I would advise you to go outside and see actually what's happening.'

Some time later, at Colonel Mohsin's invitation, I had driven to Abbottabad on my way back to the capital to join him in his spiritual home: the mess. After a tour of the extensive gardens and regimental dining room with its gleaming silverware we proceeded to the billiard room, where a portrait of the Islamic Republic's founder,

Muhammad Ali Jinnah, gazed down from the wall. This was no ordinary Jinnah. In most portraits he was misleadingly shown in Islamic dress: the sober, steely-willed founder of the nation, its first governor-general and moral light. Yet in the Frontier Force Officers' Mess, another Jinnah appeared. Cigar clenched between his teeth, he leaned over the very billiard table on which Colonel Mohsin and I now played, taking aim while a tumbler of whisky (not, judging from the evidence on the wall, his first) balanced precariously next to him. The picture had been taken many years before alcohol was banned in Pakistan. 'Ah, yes,' sighed Colonel Mohsin as he caught my eye. 'This used to be a wet bar, but since 1975 we have been dry … Wet bar, dry bar …' he repeated softly as we left the room, an untouched cup of milky tea going cold in a corner behind us.

Back on the verandah, we sat and talked and he returned to the subject of prisoners of war. Having been captured as a young lieutenant by Indian forces intervening in Bangladesh's war of liberation from West Pakistan in 1971, he had decided that it was the duty of every young officer to resist capture and to escape. With his fellow conspirators he had tunnelled vigorously to get out of the POW camp, but every tunnel had collapsed inches from the perimeter fence. 'So, after all these failed attempts to tunnel our way out, you know what we did, Tom,' he said as I shook my head. 'We made a run for it.'

Comrades in the disaster response, we embraced, shook hands and saluted as I said goodbye. A peacock wandered past the gate and I started my journey back to the capital, wondering which country and century I was in.

Years later I was stunned when 'sociable Abbottabad',

as we had known it, with its leafy streets and parks and charming markets, shot to international infamy as the final hide-out of Osama bin Laden. Introduced to the town by my friend Colonel Mohsin, I had seen it not through the lens of twenty-first-century struggles but through the perspective of another age somehow lingering, just, on the brutal frontiers of the new Great Game.

My time in the cosy and endearingly civil world of Pakistan's retired officer class was regrettably brief. 'Good morning, sunshine,' my all-too-contemporary American boss would say each day through a plume of cigarette smoke as I stumbled into the office from my cot on the floor, trying desperately to wake up. The repetition of this sardonic mantra over seven months would become almost a curse. With those words I entered the highly politicised and ruthless world of a major humanitarian operation.

The old certainties vanished instantly. To assist the people affected by the earthquake, we had to play the game, and much of this depended on what kind of guy you were. There were good guys and bad guys, cowboys, guys who 'knew their shit' and those who didn't. And there was the inevitable division between the smooth, multilingual and well-paid UN staff, known for their relative timidity in promoting humanitarian principles to Pakistan's military dictatorship, and the grotty NGO workers who glowed with self-righteousness. All complained about the honchos from headquarters, who had no idea about 'the field'. Conversations with aid workers were replete with invocations of remote gods—'Geneva knows', 'New York is watching', 'Oslo is aware'. And when the 'goodwill ambassadors' Brad Pitt and Angelina Jolie suddenly presented themselves, hardened 'grassroots' aid workers suddenly abandoned the mysterious joys of tents, drainage ditches and latrines in search of a fleeting moment of glamour.

Then there was the cast of complete weirdos—some well-intentioned, others malign—that attends major catastrophes. There was a circus troupe that travelled through the mountains trying to cheer people up, a Korean NGO promoting the health benefits of tofu consumption (with a tofu-eating cartoon character featuring, appropriately enough for an Islamic republic, a smiling pig), and the worthy but regrettably named organisation German Agro Action, which promoted recovery in the agricultural sector. And there was a series of querulous American Vietnam vets who had been given sinecures with the US government aid agency as compensation for missing limbs. Congenitally opposed to the idea of an international community and viewing the UN as some kind of communist plot, these 'one-armed bandits', as they were known, strutted and twitched their way around the province. Britain also sent its finest minds. After a long meeting with an earnest Englishwoman from the UK's Department for International Development, my boss turned to me with an acrid exhalation of cigarette smoke and growled, 'Horse's ass with teeth.'

Everyone had an agenda—personal, professional, institutional, political—and any action needed somehow to negotiate these. Institutions were at war; UN agencies and NGOs argued with each other and within themselves over responsibilities, visibility and turf. Bucks were passed and credit appropriated. Individuals on short-term emergency contracts were making connections for their next 'gig', while donors attempted to buy political favour through their generosity. Villagers were taught to say their tents were 'from the American people', and flags and logos jostled for precedence in the muddy and crowded camps that were now home to hundreds of thousands fleeing the encroaching snowline. At one meeting for the heads of the seven leading coordination agencies, I calculated 2401 permutations of vested interests and agendas that any collective decision would somehow have to navigate.

It was a desperate game of survival for not only the people affected by the earthquake but also the humanitarians. The institutional architecture for such a major international disaster response was weak and progress was dependent on the charismatic personalities who led the way. Reputations crumbled and were made; hardened aid workers went home early—shattered by the mud, the cold, the arguments and the complex logistics of the operation. One room of our office was converted into a sick bay for stricken colleagues who had caved under the pressure and needed to recuperate. 'It's like the Somme,' said one friend on his way back down from the mountains, having decided he could not continue. Gone was his earlier self-confidence; we clapped and cheered as he climbed into a helicopter waiting to take him back to the capital. He had more than done his bit, and we sensed that this mission was to be his last.

Somehow, despite the immense obstacles, pressure and confusion of the immediate aftermath of the earthquake, a coherent and effective humanitarian response emerged—more by trial and error, it seemed, than by design. And for all the follies and foibles, personalities and turf wars, it was amazing to be part of it. Alliances formed, organisations stabilised, and the initial panic, desperation and reactivity transformed into a collective purpose. It was like catching a wave: the momentum bore us along. During those months in this fascinating, politically fractured country, everyone seemed finally to think and act as one.

In the distant hills of Khala Dhaka (Black Mountain)—a tribal territory well beyond the 'writ of the state' and now the NATO frontier in an ever-expanding Afghan war—I met with groups of bearded elders wrapped in coarse woollen cloaks and smelling of wood smoke. We discussed the earthquake and its consequences in the tribal belt and beyond, and they were exceptionally well-informed—partly through their networks of tribe and extended family across Pakistan and Afghanistan, and partly from listening to the BBC Pashto Service.

We are a neutral humanitarian agency, I said. We had no politics and would only work with them if they needed and wanted us. If not, we would go away—the choice was theirs. We discussed the Green Howards (a British Army regiment), the last Europeans to have entered the area prior to the Independence and Partition of the Indian subcontinent, and I assured them I was anything but a Green Howard.

Had they been badly affected, I asked?

'*Ha*,' they replied—the guttural Pashto word for 'yes'.

Could we conduct an assessment?

'*Ha*.'

Would we be able to speak to women and children?

'*Ha*.'

Could we ensure that the most vulnerable people were assisted first?

'*Ha.*'

Would we be able to come back and monitor the aid distribution, to ensure all needs had been met?

'*Ha,*' again came the reply.

We called for green tea to cement our deal—a sign that the substantive discussions were over and that trust had been established. And then they left, each one shaking hands and embracing, walking quickly back to the Black Mountain—a distant chorus of '*Ha … Ha … Ha*' fading gently into the wood smoke and the night.

This is how we survived the earthquake—rare moments of solidarity in the turmoil of the Frontier Province—but now can we survive the drone attacks, and can we survive the war?

CHAPTER 3
FLEEING TO ISLAMABAD

'THE TIME HAS COME,' my boss said to my immense horror, 'to take on more responsibility.' I had recently finished university and had inadvertently wound up working in the banking sector. In vain, I pleaded my case—perhaps I wasn't ready, there was still so much to learn. Others had clearly shown more application and ability—was it fair for me to be chosen ahead of them? But despite my pleading I was consigned to higher duties. This was unfortunate. From my largely unsupervised administrative role, leavened by the exhilarating prospect of fortnightly pay after years of relative student penury, I was propelled into the dizzying world of the *Cheques Act 1975* and the mysteries of the Electronic Funds Code of Conduct.

Leonard was The Code Guru and felt it his duty to remind us sombrely of the days before The Code. Each provision and sub-clause was laboriously intoned aloud and accompanied by extempore interpretation in what was an almost scriptural performance. Here, the deity had been replaced by the ATM, and guidance for life's trials could be found in the diligent interpretation of the text. In those unbearably long, drab and awful hours there was The Code and beyond this lay chaos.

My promotion was a clear indication that it was time for me to leave. The evenings were spent typing up job applications and CVs, and there were exciting moments during phone interviews when I'd spend a blissful hour shouting 'What was that?' over crackly and inaudible connections from Armenia or the Congo. I sent speculative emails to any institution that looked half-decent and one day a response came back from a leading institution for conflict prevention based in Pakistan. 'Come,' it said simply, 'your desk awaits'. Elated, I booked my flights the next day.

I arrived in Islamabad at night, hot and excited. At the airport, the customs officer examined my case and asked what was in it.

'Just clothes,' I replied.

He looked at me for a second with a stern expression. 'Clean or dirty?'

'Mostly dirty.'

'That's okay, then.' He waved me through.

I had arrived, each breath of the humid night air filling my lungs with an exhilarating sense of freedom and adventure. As I stumbled around outside the airport terminal trying to find my bags and get a taxi, a haunting memory of Jawaharlal Nehru's address at the moment of Indian independence—shot in grainy footage amid the commotion and whirring fans of the parliament building in Delhi—played in my mind:

Long years ago, we made a tryst with destiny. Now the time has come when we shall redeem our pledge—not wholly or in full measure—but very substantially. At the stroke of the midnight hour, when the world sleeps, India will awake to life and freedom. A moment comes, but rarely in history, when we step out from the old to the new, when an age ends, and when the soul of a nation, long suppressed, finds utterance. It is fitting that at this solemn moment we take the pledge of dedication to the service of India and her people and to the still larger cause of humanity.

But it was 3am and I was in the wrong country. The midnight hour had long since passed and, while India had 'very substantially' redeemed its pledge at independence, Pakistan had not. Held on 14 August each year (one day before Indian independence), Pakistan's independence day celebrations were as much about independence from India as they were about independence from Britain. Despite the hope and unity contained in the new country's neologistic name—Pakistan means 'land of the pure', as well as being an acronym of the country's main constituent provinces: Punjab, Kashmir, Sindh—the trauma of Partition had been catastrophic. While it was nominally created as a homeland for the Muslim minority of the subcontinent, even today more Muslims live in India than in Pakistan. A line was drawn almost at random down the subcontinent, dissecting the great provinces of Punjab and Kashmir and cutting off cities, families and trade routes across the land. The Grand Trunk Road—which, for more than 2000 years, had connected the fabled cities of Kabul to Peshawar, Lahore, Delhi; Allahabad to Chittagong (in what was to become Bangladesh) more than 2500 kilometres away—was no longer passable. The partition of India forced the greatest mass migration of people in history, as more than 10 million Muslims, Hindus, Parsis and Sikhs left their ancestral homes and crossed the artificial borders to their new countries. Even in this most diverse of places, the barbaric imprint of the nation-state was forced onto the cosmopolitan subcontinent, causing untold violence. The abiding image of Partition is the colonial rail network, whose trains ran on schedule but arrived full of dead passengers, killed in the ethnic violence that accompanied Partition. Even Pakistan's secular founder—the brilliant Anglophile lawyer Muhammad Ali Jinnah, who perhaps did not quite realise what he had literally and metaphorically set in train by insisting on a separate Muslim homeland—described the new state as 'moth-eaten'. The sartorial reference was not misplaced: until the 1940s, when Jinnah's Muslim League began to advocate for independence, he had been seen wearing magnificently pressed linen suits, a pith helmet and a monocle. At his home in Karachi, now a museum, the state founder's personal effects are on display—luminously polished brogues are lined neatly under his bed, while the great man's cigarette holders and glittering crystal glassware are still on view. Jinnah died in 1948, little over a year after the founding of Pakistan. The elegant tailoring of the subcontinent had been ripped apart at the seams.

Pakistan in 1947 comprised two wings separated by 900 miles of Indian territory—an ethnically and linguistically homogeneous East Pakistan made up of Bengalis, and West Pakistan, dominated by the Punjab. Despite East Pakistan representing more than half of the population, it was subservient to the political and economic domination of West Pakistan, which derived much of its income and funds for industrial development from the exploitation of Bengali (East Pakistani) jute. Constitutional manipulation by both military and military-guided civilian governments sought to institutionalise the West's dominance. The underlying motivation for General Ayub Khan's 1958 military coup was to prevent the prospect of a Bengali majority in the National Assembly. With the introduction of democratic elections and the abolition of the One Unit system in 1970, the Bengali Awami League gained a healthy majority of seats in the central government to govern both West and East Pakistan. The victory of a Bengali political party in a system of government whose military, bureaucratic and economic power was predicated on the dominance of the Punjab meant that the military postponed the transfer of power. The resulting civil unrest in Bengal and the attempt to suppress opposition with the use of force led to a declaration of Bengali independence which was achieved following the India–Pakistan War in 1971. In the division of Pakistan and the creation of Bangladesh, attempts to centralise power, the neglect of both ethnic and provincial demands, and the attempt to maintain the position of the military at the expense of democratic and civilian decision-making exacerbated ethnic divisions and led to a further state partition along ethnic lines.

The scars of Partition remain. At the Wagah border between Lahore and the Sikh holy city of Amritsar sepa-rating India and Pakistan, the sixty-year confrontation is re-enacted daily. The pride of each country's armed forces—its tallest men with the shiniest boots and the loudest marching stomp face off in a carefully choreo-graphed ceremony, parading the chest-thumping asser-tion of each nation's claim to superiority. As the soldiers march at pace in a swirling mass of flying arms, legs and virulent military prowess, only the coloured turbans, which add an extra foot to the soldiers' already puffed-up pride, remain still and recognisable—the post-imperial heraldry of military menace. Trumpets sound and sergeant majors with bristling moustaches bellow commands at their strutting men, to the delight of massed crowds on either side shouting their national slogans: '*Pakistan zindabad*', '*Jai hind*'—'freedom to Pakistan', 'victory to India'. The Indian tricolour with its Ghandian spinning wheel of self-sufficiency and the green standard of Pakistan with its crescent moon are saluted and lowered in stages at exactly the same moment so that one never flies higher than the other. Bizarrely, in this orchestrated theatre of national assertion, a kind of subcontinental haka, as the flags are folded and the final commanding bellows are uttered, the two commanding officers from each side look each other in the eye and, with brisk military formality, shake hands before the vast iron gates across the continent are slammed shut. The crowds of men, women and children on either side then walk slowly towards each other—silent and calm after all the noise and display of the soldiers— and look with curiosity at the exotic species on the other side, separated by a few metres and a wire fence. No one talks, no one waves—it is as if they have woken up for the first time in years, blinked and encountered themselves in the mirror, slightly older, utterly recognisable, and not quite the xenophobes, fundamentalists and vengeful ideologues that either side has been led to expect.

Even in the curiously antiquated language of radio call signs—whose tangos, romeos and foxtrots echo the jaunty language of World War II Spitfire pilots—the Indo-Pakistan rivalry made itself felt. In the Islamic Republic, *I for India* was unacceptable (replaced with the more neutral *Italy*) while *W for Whisky* remained in place, much joked about by the country's Johnny Walker–quaffing officer class.

At Partition, Pakistan was left with the rump of the country: half of Punjab, half of Kashmir and the depopulated and troubled frontier provinces of Balochistan and the North West Frontier. Aside from the city of Lahore, and perhaps Peshawar, this new state created for the subcontinent's Muslim population was cut off from the great centres of South Asian Islam: Delhi and Agra with their Red Forts and the Taj Mahal; Aligarh, whose university was modelled on the Oxford colleges where many of Pakistan's leaders were educated, and was where the idea of 'the land of the pure' was born; Lucknow, the courtly cultural capital of the Urdu-speaking world. These places were now in India—a new and different country.

The experience of Partition was one of both logic and lunacy combined—the logic of the ethno-nationalist

31

nation-state chaotically superimposed over the entire Indian subcontinent. The creation of Pakistan embodied this strange contradiction: it was an ancient neologism; a country for the Muslim minority that contained only a minority of the subcontinent's Muslims; and its source of life—the river Indus—gave name to the state from which the creators of Pakistan sought to escape.

Even Pakistan's national language was not widely spoken in the truncated lands that would become Pakistan. Urdu (related to the word 'horde') was a language of Northern India, a military lingua franca that arose out of the army camps of the former Mughal Empire. It is largely the same as Hindi but written in the Arabic script and more heavily influenced by an Arabic and Persian vocabulary. The Urdu-speaking Northern Indians who migrated to Pakistan after 1947, who became the country's military and administrative elite, were known within Pakistan as *mohajir*, a term derived from the Arabic word meaning 'immigrant'.

When I had arrived in Islamabad, the capital created by such *mohajirs*, I did not realise the power this association held and did not become aware of it until I started organising a trip into the rural Punjab to observe local elections. The Punjabis—the most populous group in Pakistan—had seen their written language banned at Partition and the compulsory expansion of Urdu as the language of state, as artificial and remote from the earthy ribaldry of Punjabi as the capital itself. Calling random government offices, electoral departments and district commissioners, I was told of a slightly longer than usual crackle over the ancient phone lines as it dawned on the local administrators in their dusty, paper-strewn offices, that they were being summoned from the capital. Any and every request was agreed to instantly with an unhesitating 'yes, Sir' as representatives from the capital expressed their seigneurial rights: cars, accommodation, food, guides, information were all supplied without question. Getting off the phone after another of these calls to an unsuspecting minor official, a colleague of mine once remarked that he 'could hear his spine stiffen.' Just receiving a call out of the blue from a member of the Urdu-speaking elite in the capital had terrified him.

The brilliant Urdu short-story writer Saadat Hasan Manto wrote heart-rendingly about the moment of Partition, expressing much of the bewilderment and absurdity of the moment—a sensation that can still accompany new arrivals in Islamabad. His bleakly comic story 'Toba Tek Singh' is set in a lunatic asylum during the creation of the two new states and the administrative difficulties in working out which countries each of the inmates should belong to. One Sikh lunatic asks, 'Why are we being sent to India? We don't even know what language they speak there,' while a Muslim inmate shouts '*Pakistan zindabad*' with such vigour that he loses his balance, falls over and is knocked out. The new boundaries cause endless confusion. 'If they were in India, where on earth was Pakistan? And if they were in Pakistan, then how come that until only the other day it was India?' Another inmate escapes and seeks sanctuary from the lunacy of Partition itself by climbing a tree, declaring: 'I wish to live neither in India nor in Pakistan. I wish to live in this tree.' Two Anglo-Indian lunatics are concerned that the European ward in the asylum will be abolished, that breakfast will never be served again and they will be forced to eat chapattis. There is general concern that, in the confusion of Partition, both India and Pakistan would simply slide off the map altogether.

Despite its relative newness as a country, Pakistan is a land with a long, troubled and somewhat truncated history—and is influenced by the great civilisations with which it borders: Afghanistan, Iran, China and India. So much of what is now written about Pakistan ignores this—it is seen as a piece on the geopolitical chessboard, a difficult ally, a hard place, the most dangerous place on earth, prone to extremism and facing sectarian meltdown. The idea of Pakistan has become synonymous with threats posed by supposed 'Talibanisation' and 'atomic mullahs'.

One day, while walking through the narrow, windy streets of Peshawar's old city, I was stopped by a man in long white robes, with dark glasses and a long black beard. Having been taught to be suspicious of precisely this stereotype, I started our conversation guardedly. We discussed the weather (hot), the cricket (dull), tourist sites in and around Peshawar. Just as I was beginning to wonder what the catch was, the man gripped me by the hand and shook it vigorously. 'You see,' he said, 'we are not all terrorists.' And we went our separate ways. Now that Pakistan is increasingly seen as Afpak—part of the front line in the war in Afghanistan—it is almost radical to suggest that its overwhelming social, cultural, political and economic ties lie with an Indic, rather than Talibanic, civilisation.

Daylight, as always, cast its tepid light over the heady exultation of my night-time arrival in Islamabad. The city was very far from what I had imagined. It was not the thriving subcontinental metropolis of 'life and liberty' that I had imagined from the glorious words of Nehru's speech. In his own address to the nation on 15 August 1947, Pakistan's founder, Muhammad Ali Jinnah, in well-intentioned but less inspired rhetoric, said:

> *Our object should be peace within and peace without. We want to live peacefully and maintain cordial and friendly relations with our immediate neighbors and with the world at large. We have no aggressive designs against any one. We stand by the United Nations Charter and will gladly make our full contribution to the peace and prosperity of the world.*

The city of Islamabad was the incarnation of Jinnah's view—a lawyers' creation given form by a military love of order and right angles, thus giving urban expression to two of the dominant forces of Pakistan's post-independence history: the army and the judiciary. Its order and tranquillity did not breathe the excitement of the midnight hour but reflected 'an opportunity to demonstrate to the world how can a nation, containing many elements, live in peace and amity and work for the betterment of all its citizens, irrespective of caste or creed', as Jinnah described the mission of his new nation. Islamabad did just this.

I woke to wide empty boulevards and leafy suburbs. Vast houses lined the road next to the Margalla Hills, the foothills of the Himalayas, and a neatly trimmed cricket pitch with a gabled pavilion glinted in the early morning sun. The city, as I discovered, was one vast urban grid of order and logic, trees and gardens, and neat designated shopping zones whose air-conditioned shops sold rich fabrics, books, and knocked-off designer goods. Advertising hoardings promoted Coke and mobile phone companies offering to 'connect the gentry'. I wandered round, slightly bewildered by this almost-empty Islamic Canberra, whose suburbs had been given alphanumeric sequences of sectors and subsectors instead of names. The main shopping centre was in F10, while my hotel languished in the obscurity of E7/2. The vast government boulevard named after the former Chinese premier Zhou Enlai was a modern concrete rendition of Lutyens's Delhi. Ever grander buildings culminated in what was known as Benazir's house, or the Pink Palace—a colossal pseudo-Mughal building in soft pink marble and sandstone built to accommodate the political aspirations and realisations of the Bhutto family. Where in Britain and Australia the mark of the arriviste financier was mock-Tudor, in Pakistan it was mock-Mughal; not quaint homeliness but the mausolean splendour of the Taj Mahal.

After a morning walking around and talking to nobody, I returned to my hotel room, with its exceptionally loud and ineffective air conditioner, the soothingly bland predictability of BBC World and pictures of eighteenth-century English rural scenes—pheasants taking flight, a man (with top hat and tails) and a woman (in a lacy dress) admiring a swan. There I pondered my findings. Thinking I would use this momentary reprieve to try to learn some Urdu, I had a look at a teach-yourself language book but was slightly put off by such chapter headings as 'I do not have a reservation' and 'Where's my wife?'.

With all its separateness and control, Islamabad did not so much present an example of modernity and progress to the rest of the world as repeat the follies of the old. In all cities in the subcontinent there exists the 'old city', with its swirling streets and vibrant centres whose lanes are filled with lives and livelihoods exhibited to the world from small shopfronts and market stalls that—to the outsider—wind their way in a mesmerising knot of chaos and commerce. Beyond this, the colonial rulers established the cantonment or the civil lines catering to an altogether new imperial reality. Where the great Mughal mosques, palaces and centres of government were located at the heart of undivided India's great cities, the British rule introduced a separation, especially after the mass uprising against British rule in 1857, variously known as the sepoy rebellion, the Indian Mutiny or the First War of Independence. Virtually all towns and cities in India and Pakistan thus have civil lines or a cantonment once reserved for the British army and bureaucracy but now occupied by the Pakistani middle class and retired military officers, whose rents were becoming increasingly exorbitant. During an early visit to find cheap accommodation in Islamabad, accompanied by a friend's contact in the Islamabad real estate world, I even managed to pass out at precisely the moment when yet another venal landlord started his quotes—this time for a mini oven masquerading as a room.

Islamabad, I realised, was the cantonment to the thriving city of Rawalpindi. Built as the model city of the new state it had, in fact, replicated a much older version of imperial rule equally marked by the social and administrative separateness of the new (military) ruling elites.

A few weeks later, and after a few more visits to Rawalpindi, I sought to impress a young Austrian diplomat with my knowledge of the swirling chaos of Rawalpindi and to entice her away from ordered and highly fortified mini-Switzerland of Islamabad's diplomatic enclave, I suggested a date in 'pindi with exaggerated promises of adventure and the 'real Pakistan'. Leaving behind the world of red number plates, expat-only embassy clubs, and official cars marked with ceremonial swords strapped to their bonnets, we took a local bus in forty-five degree heat into the heart of Pakistan's other capital and immediately got lost in the maze of ancient streets and covered bazaars. I had attempted to make an effort and had recently bought some local clothes—a lightly decorated linen shalwar kameez—and hoped to blend in, or at least not to stand out too badly. The sun was intense and my misguided resistance to sunscreen and hats had led my colleagues at the office to call me gulabi sahib (pink sir) rather than gora sahib (white sir), which Europeans were usually called, on account of my regular sunburn. Trying to impress with my sense of local style and to offset the disadvantages of pale skin, I donned my new finery and set foot tentatively into the crowded bus with my date. The response was electric—our fellow passengers erupted into applause, slapped me on the back, offered congratulations and, as the bus lurched down the street an itinerant imam offered to convert me to Islam on the spot. Slowly it dawned on me that I had bought not an ordinary shalwar kameez but a marriage suit and the other passengers had come to the conclusion that we were traveling to Rawalpindi to tie the knot!

In 'pindi itself, the response on the street was equally cheerful and my attempt to blend in suddenly became a mock-nuptial procession with cheering, well wishes, invitations to tea and the imam in tow, determined not to let pass his opportunity to save souls. This was too much for the Austrian who was immediately ill-at-ease amid the crowds, stares, ribald humour, and momentary celebrity caused by my sartorial confusion. We briefly took refuge in an abandoned Hindu temple next a street vendor selling cool, freshly crushed pomegranate juice and contemplated our next move. Knowing that the covered Rajah Bazaar was nearby where there were likely to be more women and she would feel less exposed, I suggested that we plunge into the arrhythmic mesh of side streets and make for the bazaar. It was a fatal move. If we had been lost before, within moments we had become dreadfully entangled, not in the cool of the bazaar itself looking at exotic fabrics and making memorable tourist purchases, but in the depths of the Rawalpini meat-market. It was fascinatingly awful—street after narrow street was lined with carts and hole-in-the-wall butcheries choking with diesel fumes, flies, dust and the smell of meat turning progressively more rancid in the midday sun. The dirt paths were splattered and puddled with blood and off-cuts and around us were the convulsing bodies of newly slaugh-tered animals. Promising that I knew the way out, I led her around a corner only to come face-to-face with a dead end and another grim series of shops whose great meat-hooks prominently displayed their treasured wares: bulls testicles swinging sickeningly in the smog-filled afternoon breeze.

Used to the hyper-cleanliness of Vienna supermarkets, my companion was deeply unimpressed and, as a vege-tarian, was understandably incensed. She had by now come to the realisation that my claims to know 'pindi's complex geography, made in the safety of the Islamabad's diplomatic enclave, may not have been altogether accurate. To the amazement of the onlookers who had moments before been wishing us a happy wedding, an argument erupted with each of us claiming the other had been misled. And there, in my wedding attire covered in blood, sweat, flies and pollution, I realised that I had inadvertently found myself in the polar opposite of the sanitised cantonment world of Islamabad. While my date may have ended in disaster, my Pakistan journey had started exhilaratingly.

CHAPTER 4
POLITICS OF THE
'PROLETARIAN LUNCH'

'LET'S GO SOMEWHERE really proletarian for lunch today,'
said Imran, rubbing his hands with delight as he emerged
from his office—a glorified compression chamber of
ancient newspapers and harsh cigarette smoke sweetened
with hashish. I smiled wanly as my early enthusiasm for
these 'proletarian lunches' of dhal and chapattis, or sometimes just cigarettes and the occasional joint, had worn
away under successive bouts of food poisoning. Grimacing
and bracing myself for another nauseating round of ined-
ible street food, I dutifully followed Imran out of the quiet
and chilly comfort of the highly air-conditioned office
and out onto the street. Even going out onto the street
in the full heat of the summer (at least 45 degrees with
high humidity) defied both the weather and the accepted

conventions of the Pakistani middle class. These lunches, for all their gastrointestinal cost, had become vital in my political education in Pakistan.

My daily work as a would-be analyst of Pakistani affairs involved reading the newspapers from cover to cover in the morning and going out to extended lunches with gossipy, well-connected friends from the office or the coterie of analysts and purveyors of political intrigue, who seemed to fill every corner of Islamabad. This was followed by more reading about Pakistan's political complexities in the afternoon. In the evenings, over al fresco dinners at the Kabul Restaurant, we would hatch yet more exotic conspiracies before buying up pirated DVDs and heading back to the minute flat I shared with another apprentice analyst to watch, spellbound, as the great Bollywood screen sirens Aishwarya Rai and Madhuri Dixit wove their majestic way through historical melodramas set in the Muslim north of the subcontinent before Partition. It was, if nothing else, an extremely intense crash course in subcontinental politics, culture and history of the most intoxicating kind—an excitement only heightened by the fact that I was able to spend a reasonable amount of time out by myself travelling in Peshawar, Karachi and Lahore, where I had the opportunity to meet and interview many of the main protagonists from the political, military, diplomatic and NGO worlds.

Being effectively a local institution, rather than the embodiment of a big international NGO, we had much greater freedom. There was no security and no restrictions, and I was free to do more or less as I pleased. The other huge advantage was that, in an expatriate world in which there is often a tendency towards self-aggrandisement and complaint about local people and conditions, I worked in an organisation staffed and run by some of brightest Pakistanis of their generation. These were people who had studied and taught at the world's leading universities, each of them fluent in half a dozen European and Asian languages, and who casually reminisced about addressing congresses and parliaments and dining with presidents and foreign ministers. They did so on the basis of extensive field work in extremely demanding conditions so as to advocate the cause of peace. Theirs was a deep sophistication and when, later on, I was lucky enough to work with what I now realise was one of the finest European NGOs around, my reaction was to find my new colleagues personally and intellectually boorish by comparison, as evenings of discussion and historical melodrama were replaced with the consumption of beer and a chewing tobacco beloved of Scandinavians, called snus. (As these evenings progressed, my interlocutors found their ability to communicate impaired by a small teabag of tobacco that was stuffed under the upper lip. This left a brown stain down the front right incisor tooth; like cultish mafia tattoo, it was the clear and unambiguous mark of the Scandinavian aid worker.) In Pakistan, after being a very small and largely ineffectual cog in a very large Australian bank, I suddenly felt that I'd made it to the centre of the universe in which everything was urgent and new and stimulating.

We referred to our office as 'Sweden'—a homage to a character in the brilliant novel *Moth Smoke* by Pakistani writer Mohsin Hamid. In it, an inspirational teacher at Lahore University, Professor Perfect, outlines a climatic political economy of Pakistan. The separation between the elite and the masses previously exhibited in the cantonments and in the civil lines of Islamabad had evolved into the invisible apartheid of climate control. While the masses sweated it out in the stifling humidity of the streets, the urban elites lived in an arctic luxury closely approximating, according to Professor Perfect, the climate of Sweden—sharing literally nothing in common with the rest of the population, not even the temperature. Going out for a daily 'proletarian lunch' therefore became an act of rebellion against the prevailing order. Imran's car (itself a mass grave of dead flies and the dying garlands of jasmine flowers bought from children on the street) sped us away to obscure roadside shacks where charcoal braziers reheated thick clumps of dhal garnished with enormous quantities of chilli and small rocks. In one particularly bohemian establishment, located under a nearby juniper tree, no food was ever forthcoming, but the sheltered location provided an opportunity for what in Pakistan passed for a liquid lunch—foul-smelling joints that suppressed hunger and fuelled ever more elaborate and incomprehensible political conspiracy theories.

But mainly the conversations returned again and again to cricket. In true irony, only in Pakistan, a nominally dry Muslim country, was Australian cricketer David Boon a celebrity and whose world record of the number of tinnies consumed on the flight from Sydney to London (fifty-two) widely known. 'How is the "keg on legs"?' asked Imran in our first meeting, lighting up yet another acrid Chester-field cigarette, clearly fancying himself as a sort of subcontinental version of the ocker batsman.

Imran was in the older tradition of Pakistani radical—a figure who might have been more at home in the heady days of Zulfikar Ali Bhutto rather than Benazir or the succession of conservative generals who held power following her father's execution. Imran's was a populist and socialist tradition, entirely secular (although not totally indifferent to Sufi traditions as long as they were accompanied by music and marijuana), whose equal dislike of both the increasingly conservative religion of the Urdu-speaking middle class, from which he came, and the Sweden-dwelling upper orders whose education he shared, put him at odds with much of contemporary Pakistan. In the exclusive Islamabad clubs and receptions he would embarrass his hosts by speaking in Urdu—which was simply not done by the upper orders, for whom knowledge of English, and in some cases Persian, was paramount. At the same time he had a horror of the growing religious conservatism at the heart of daily life.

Since Imran was a child, the relative secularism of early Pakistan had begun to change and even common expressions were being given increasingly religious overtones. To say 'goodbye', it was becoming frowned upon to use the traditional Urdu expression *khuda hafiz*, borrowed from the Persian, meaning 'God protect you' but without specifying whose or which god was being referred to, thus creating room for religious plurality. Instead, the new term *Allah hafiz* had been introduced during the 1980s by the deeply religious military ruler Zia ul Haq who, with CIA support, was sponsoring a nascent Taliban (then styled as 'freedom fighters') against the Soviet Union in Afghanistan. This new term was religiously specific and was emblematic, for Imran, of Pakistan's turn away from its Indo-Persian cosmopolitan traditions towards a stricter and more conservative religious public culture.

In its urban design and planning, Islamabad had started as a secular representation of the new republic but even this was beginning to change. At some intersections day labourers lined the streets and were hired and fed by Islamic organisations seeking influence through welfare, in a deeply corrupt state where this was never likely to be provided. Beards lengthened, and the daily line-ups took place increasingly close to the main shopping centres and playgrounds of the capital's more westernised consumer classes, gradually influencing the tone and public culture. Around Jinnah Super Market, one of the main dining and shopping precincts in Islamabad, bearded men lined up every Friday on an unclaimed patch of land near the shops to pray. Soon they were doing this daily, and before long a concrete base was constructed to accommodate them. Clearly this was the first step in the construction of a new mosque in the centre of the market, casting a shadow of sobriety and puritanism over the place where the city's fashionable men and women gathered on hot evenings. Unspoken and unchallenged, this subtle religious encroachment into a secular materialist world advertising mobile phones, soft drinks, music, DVDs, colourful and fashionable clothes, offering opportunities for men and women to walk, talk, shop and eat together suggested a broader struggle for competing visions of the future of Pakistan.

Western observers had consistently seen the army as the guarantee of a pro-capitalist secular social order against perceptions of increasing religious radicalism, although here too concerns existed about the extent of religious infiltration of the rank and file. When I asked Imran about this, he rolled his eyes. Among the more bizarre activities of the international diplomatic corps and would-be spies was the annual 'beard count' during the military parades on independence day. Here, trained analysts scrutinised the country's armed forces for facial hair, carefully noting its frequency, length and, if possible, the degree to which it was 'Islamic' in cut, in a foolhardy effort to gauge the religious and political sympathies of Pakistan's dominant political institution: the army. After much comparison, the follicular analysis (or beard count) usually came up with the same figure: 15 per cent.

CHAPTER 5
ELECTIONEERING IN THE PUNJAB

A BATTERED JEEP with green Government of Punjab number plates pulled up outside the bus station in the town of Mandi Bahauddin and a henna-haired driver, apparently twitching with fleas, jumped out and announced that he would be with me twenty-four hours a day, touring polling booths. Pakistan's local elections were taking place and I had been asked by the research organisation I was working for to go as an election monitor and report on how voting was conducted in the rural Punjab. I had tried to register formally with the government as an election observer, but a particularly intense bout of food poisoning following another of Imran's lunches had prevented me from presenting myself before the authorities. This may have been quite fortunate, as it turned out. I had been living in

Pakistan under largely false pretences on a series of short-term tourist visas that I would get renewed every few months. My regular appearances before the immigration officials in Islamabad had begun to cause much administrative amusement as I invented ever more outlandish tourist plans in order to justify yet another visa extension. 'You must have seen almost all of Pakistan by now,' said one of the officials as I turned up begging for another three months. For a nerve-wracking moment, as I envisaged my Pakistan experience ending in deportation, I struggled for an excuse that was in some way different from the last one and hopefully more plausible. As I coughed and stuttered in search of inspiration, the immigration official sensed my panic and gently suggested, 'Perhaps you haven't seen the mountains in Gilgit and Skardu yet—they are well worth visiting.' With a wry smile he stamped my passport for three more months. Perhaps he knew and had maintained the charade: whatever the answer to the question 'reason for visit' on the visa form, 'self-appointed international election observer' was only going to get me kicked out. As I scrambled into the jeep, I was getting deeper into Pakistan's political nightmare than I ever imagined: the local elections that year were marred by gerrymandering, government favouritism, and extensive rigging including ballot stuffing, intimidation and seizure of voting stations. Sixty people were killed and more than five hundred were injured.

Since its first military coup d'état in 1958, Pakistan has been ruled either directly or indirectly by military governments. Despite recurring elections, on no occasion has the incumbent political party been voted out of office, and transfers of power have always been preceded by military interventions. Pakistan's last three elected prime ministers—Zulfikar Ali Bhutto, Benazir Bhutto and Nawaz Sharif—were either executed or exiled. General Pervez Musharraf seized power in a bloodless coup from Nawaz Sharif in 1999 before being ousted himself following a crisis of constitutional legitimacy when he attempted to unseat the powerful and influential chief justice of Pakistan, Iftikhar Muhammad Chaudhry. Perversely, Pakistan's military regimes justified their takeover of power in order re-establish 'genuine' democracy. In his first address to the nation on assuming power, Musharraf stated: 'The armed forces have no intention of staying in charge any longer than is absolutely necessary to pave the way for true democracy to flourish in Pakistan'.

In the first local elections since the last military coup, the process was designed not to choose democratically who would govern in local politics but sought to remove the power of provincial governments and to undercut the electoral basis for political opposition to military rule. Under a devolution plan, 'grassroots' democracy was presented as a substitute for democratisation at national and provincial levels. The purpose of devolution to local government was to depoliticise governance, create a new political elite that would undermine established political opposition, demonstrate democratic legitimacy to internal and external audiences, and undermine the federal principle in which the political, administrative and fiscal autonomy of the provinces was constitutionally guaranteed. Furthermore, the devolution plan also gave the military control of the administrative functions of local government, and extended military influence into the bureaucracy.

As the jeep roared off, its loose rear door swinging wildly every time we turned a corner, Imran and I carefully studied an electoral map of the town that had been given to me by the local police commissioner. On it were marked the council constituencies and, in red, the areas that were most likely to be politically and physically contested. Deciding not to waste our time on uncontroversial seats, we headed straight for the red zones—a slightly foolhardy decision, as it turned out, because one of Imran's relatives was also running for office.

The elections were hot, dusty and marked by silent lines of patient voters and moments of bad temper. During the night we followed the campaign trail of Imran's cousin as he and his father made their way through the town, holding court at an old cinema the family once owned (now closed owing to the government's heavy-handed and puritan censorship) or on string beds set up under trees to catch the cool, sweet breeze of the Punjabi night. The process was interminable and was an exercise in patronage, influence and ultimately in the power of relationships that were as much intergenerational alliances as they were voting preferences—a far cry from the momentary and insincere pressing of the flesh at train stations and in shopping centres that passes for campaigning in the West. While it was the young men, the sons, who were nominally standing for the local mayoral positions, it was their fathers who were behind their campaigns, dispensing influence, staying out all night discussing life, family and politics at the various nocturnal rendezvous points around the city, and adding their personal and financial weight and gravitas to the political aspirations of the next generation. It was a dynastic system—the family business interests were clearly more important than entering politics, and so the male head of the household stayed out of the running to ensure that the more dispensable first sons would become their pliable government representatives. At the street meetings and in dealing with potential voters, Imran's cousin, who was nominally running for office, would sit slightly behind and to the side of his father in silence, nervously fingering his newly grown moustache. Early hopes were high—he had selected a soccer ball as his symbol and it was thought, given the popularity of the sport, that this would give him an edge among illiterate voters.

After a night on the streets drinking sickly sweet milky tea and smoking innumerable cigarettes with the campaign supporters, I crashed into bed—a foam mattress on the floor—only to be woken a few hours later for another campaign meeting with the offer of a thick slug of Johnny Walker. As I wheezed back to life I felt more like a character in a hard-boiled political thriller than the diligent and impartial election observer that I had set out to be.

The crunch of my boots on the gravel woke the driver of the jeep and, suddenly conscious again, he started his eternal fight against the fearful fleas—constantly twitching, scratching and contorting even while at the wheel of the speeding jeep as it veered through crowded markets and down narrow backstreets. Most of the polling booths in the electoral red zone were segregated women's polling stations. Allegedly, manipulation of men's polling stations was potentially more violent and carried greater risk, so the various sides focussed on corrupting the women's vote. The men's polling stations were generally run quite well—long silent lines of men queued for their chance to tick a name on a list (or at least identify a face or a symbol if they could not read the name) and the proceedings seemed a model of propriety until, looking at the ballots themselves in a back room, I realised that a large number of them had already been filled in. The men were being given the opportunity to vote freely in a well-organised and respectful process in which the outcome had already been decided.

The women's polling stations were considerably more chaotic. Imran was constantly questioned about his identity and was threatened with being kicked out despite being officially registered with the government as an observer. I had no trouble at all, however, despite having been too ill to fill out the official paperwork. 'BBC!' people shouted as I walked into the polling stations and was granted access to everyone and everything despite being a total imposter, while Imran, the official observer, struggled to get in. And, as a foreigner to whom the conventional rules did not apply, I walked straight into the electoral catastrophe of Pakistan's women's polling stations.

Progress was slow and long lines of women, some with children, formed in the growing heat of the day. Here, the authorities hadn't bothered with prior manipulations of the ballots but used intimidation to ensure that people voted the 'right' way. The wife of the main mayoral candidate stood over the ballot box, interrogating each of the voters as they approached and examining their ballot. She was an intimidating figure, dressed in a red shalwar kameez and presiding over the ballot box. Each voter, after waiting interminably in line, had to walk up a short flight of steps and stand below the mayor's wife—humbly offering their vote as a kind of subservient tribute rather than an instrument of political choice, power and expression. She ran the show impassively, having completely sidelined the electoral officer, who sat a nearby desk. When Imran and I asked what she thought was going on and requested that she intervene, the electoral officer shrugged her shoulders as if encountering a mildly irritating fly. The mayor's wife was equally unmoved. At this electoral station, voting was not a expression of choice but an act of propriety, the main candidates seeing the votes of their constituents as nothing more than their due.

The process was interminable and, as the sun reached its zenith, conditions in the small, crowded, uncovered schoolyard began to deteriorate. People started passing out and were left where they had collapsed, or clutched their heads while curled up against the wall to get out of the sun. Unable to intervene because of cultural sensitivities around touching women, I went to get a member of the special all-female police force to lift those who had collapsed in the shade. For the rest of the time I ceased my electoral observation work and carried water to the voters who had crashed against the side wall, while trying to keep a eye on the antics of the mayor's wife. Imran was enraged at the blatant fraud that was taking place before our eyes—this was his country, not mine, and the blatant manipulations and standover tactics were intolerable. A discussion with the local police officer followed, in which we both intervened and requested that the ballot boxes be protected from influence so that people could vote without immediate intimidation. The police were reluctant to intervene, at which point Imran took up the issue directly with the mayor's wife, who wouldn't be moved but did manage to hold up polling even more. As the argument developed, there was angry shouting from the gate and the mayor himself burst in to the compound, followed by his henchmen, as word had clearly got out that the polling station wasn't quite the stitch-up he had imagined. There followed an enormous argument with the female police officers, who said he couldn't enter the compound owing to the existing segregation principles. He ignored them and rounded on Imran, telling him to get out. The hairy accomplices leered at us both. For some reason, as the tension mounted, I decided to get out my camera again and start recording the moment—at this point someone else yelled out 'BBC!' and the intensity of the moment shifted. Strangely, the erroneous utterance of the broadcaster had changed the dynamic in the courtyard. We had gone from being on the verge of being beaten up to a steely but stand-offish confrontation. Perhaps also the mayor had realised that his job had been done. Among the screaming children and the collapsed bodies of voters in the yard, no one would have been prepared to vote any other way than the prescribed one. Imran and I stayed on till the end. The mayor's wife had long since disappeared, and while the rest of the election had proceeded relatively smoothly, the message about political power had been rammed home. Wherever it lay, it was certainly not with the female voters of the Punjab. The 'BBC' would come and go and, with the best of intentions, Imran and I had only brought the unspoken calculus of the political system into the open momentarily, and it had been vain to hope that we could have done anything else. In the counting, which we stayed on to witness, the mayor was re-elected almost unopposed.

But this was not the case at the men's polling stations.

By 2am most of the ballot boxes had been delivered to the district returning officer, and we stood around watching the count. After a short break for prayers and cigarettes the counting resumed, and this time the fathers gathered around the returning officer to see what fate their sons had in store. Heads shook and beards waggled as votes were counted in the heat of the night, and then the chorus of 'bogus vote, bogus vote' echoed into the evening—the returning officer had clearly come across the pre-filled ballot from the men's polling stations. Tension mounted in the room and a roar went up among the supporters outside—the remaining ballot boxes had just arrived in a car belonging to one of the candidates, a soccer ball clearly visible on the outside of the car.

Most of the supporters were armed—and politics, despite the gentlemanly conduct in front of the returning officer, was highly factional. I looked at Imran and he produced a small envelope we had been given before we left Islamabad on our mission. 'Only open this if there is a serious problem,' we had been told. It seemed to us that being surrounded by armed and angry supporters of a candidate who had just discovered the obvious and overt extent of electoral rigging constituted such a scenario. Imran tore open the envelope and produced a small card: *In case of emergency ring the duty manager in Brussels during working hours.* AK-47 shots were fired—whether in anger or in triumph—into the night.

CHAPTER 6
A SECOND HIMALAYAN WINTER

WHILE AID HAD POURED in for the earthquake, a year later a smaller but in many ways nastier emergency presented itself. I had stayed on through the summer in Pakistan after the first earthquake and had continued to work with aid agencies on the longer-term humanitarian and recovery efforts. I had witnessed the frenetic activity of the first response, followed by a gradual diminishing of the aid effort as the weather slowly improved. Aid agencies had left along with their resources and personnel and with them, the vast amounts of information and intimate knowledge of the small villages and hamlets of Pakistan's North seeped away—lost to the grinding juggernaut of official long-term development planning. The imperatives of immediate practical action had given way to the bigger politics of reconstruction loans, strategies and policies that were negotiated not from small towns but in distant centres of political and economic power in Washington, Brussels and Islamabad. Eager to demonstrate that normality had returned and the recovery effort was well underway, the government had put a freeze on emergency shelter programs, and donors had largely drifted away. This left World Bank consultants to develop outlandish plans for earthquake-resistant houses made from reinforced concrete and brick, in the mountains where people had traditionally used only mud and timber—a plan met with great enthusiasm by Pakistan's military government, whose retired generals and officers managed the country's army-owned construction and engineering companies. Earthquake reconstruction promised to be an economic boon if billions in reconstruction funds based on plans hatched in Washington and Islamabad were to go ahead.

Many of the people displaced by the earthquake had returned home, but a small population of about 40,000 people remained in residual camps across the North West Frontier and Kashmir. There had been significant government pressure for them to leave, out of a totally misplaced fear of 'aid dependency' and conviction that the authorities had the situation in hand. It was often a case of disappearing camps—monitoring teams would report that a site they had visited the day before, a thriving community, had been bulldozed and no one knew where the people had gone. Despite repeated calls for a more cooperative response to the residual camps, allowing people time and giving them information about their options (if there were any), the pace of camp destruction continued. My counterpart, the Commissioner for Camps, was normally the Commissioner for Afghan Refugees, a position that afforded him considerable influence over trade between the two countries, and he was keen to return to his more lucrative day job. For him, the residuals were both a blot on the relief effort and an impediment to obtaining greater riches.

I had grown to like the camps, and would sometimes walk through the nearest ones at night when I had finished work or needed a break. Although they were crowded with people housed in poor-quality tents, I found something almost reassuring about passing through the nightly rituals of family life after the frenetic work of the day. Fires were lit, lights were on, people talked in the warmth of the evening and fascinatingly, for a country in which domestic life is so closed to anyone beyond the immediate extended family, they offered me the chance to glimpse behind the scenes.

But another emergency was waiting. The camps and the tents had been put up quickly following the earthquake, and a year later people still lived under the now-worn canvas. In Australia, for people to still be living under canvas more than a few days after a major disaster was seen as a failure of the state response, but in Pakistan families of five to seven people had been living in tents for almost twelve months. While most had tried to go back, these people could not— entire villages had been swept away in a deluge of earth and there were no homes to return to; some were tenants who no longer had land tenure, others had had their livelihoods or farmlands destroyed. These were no malingerers, and in any case the camps were no place to stay if there was any other viable option. Those in the decrepit residual camps now faced a second winter under canvas with even less than they'd had during the immediate emergency response, and with a freeze on further relief activity. The apparent pleasures of family life on long summer evenings were a temporary reprieve: in a few months' time the camp would become water-logged mud pits with shelters that could not conceivably withstand the harshness of the Himalayan winter.

One of the frequent visitors to our office was a representative from a small Italian education NGO that was providing food, shelter and ongoing education to children who had lost everything—a vital attempt to stave off the longer-term loss of opportunity and 'development gains' that disasters bring in their wake. In her perfect Italian-inflected English, my friend Alberta would storm in and demand, 'What about the children?' I tried to help by supplying her NGO with the relief provisions we had—clothes, blankets, roofing materials, tents, hygiene kits, water purifiers, anything that we could provide. But it was difficult—response is in many ways an economy of scale and, collectively, we were trying to assist 700,000 people across the North West Frontier. While drawing up relief distribution plans for hundreds of thousands of items, Alberta's requests were very specific. When a shipment of 50,000 sets of assorted children's clothes came through, Alberta appeared in the office.

'I want thirty-four,' she said adamantly.

'For fuck's sake, Alberta,' I intemperately replied, 'can't you at least take five hundred?'

The average family size was estimated at 7.44 and we were aiming for 'coverage' of the entire population, which did not generally cater for specific needs. But she insisted, rightly, and putting the dictates of the majority aside we packed and repacked until she had the exact number.

Possibly the worst moments in the battle between generic

large-scale response and individual needs was when people would come to our door with petitions. Often these were damp, stained, handwritten notes with stories of personal tragedy or lists of households and family names of people who had lost their homes. Some we were able to re-direct but others were turned away.

'I'm sorry but we can't help individuals,' I was told. 'They need at least to be assessed.' There were genuine fears that if we stared handing out relief items there were thousands more people who could appear at our gate and we would have no means of responding. Human misery, as always, appears between systemic cracks.

When serving the interests of a majority—the 'target population for coverage', in humanitarian jargon—some individual cases became emblematic of the situation. We heard reports of a girl who had a broken spine and was lying in a tent in an unspecified location in Pakistan's North. The story was repeated and shocked everyone. The Pakistan Army commander for the response in the North West Frontier province even cried at a public meeting when he heard it, and army units were dispatched to locate her. A German medical team scoured the district but, while the story had been vivid in its depiction of suffering, it was vague on specifics. Who was this girl? Where were her parents? Where, in fact, was she? In the end we concluded that the story was probably an unsubstantiated rumour but somehow it captured the worst fear of responders— that in trying to reach everyone, numbers became more important than names and real needs could be missed. By the end of the winter there was 97 per cent 'coverage' and no 'reported incidence of increased morbidity' as a consequence of the earthquake. 'These mountain people are tough' was a common refrain in the aid community, but was this resilience or was life just incredibly tenuous in Himalayan poverty at the best of times?

Strangely, for relaxation during those precious few hours after work I would sit in my room in front of a two-bar electric heater and read Primo Levi—an Italian chemist who applied his scientific brilliance to describing the fundamental elements of human experience of Auschwitz in his piercing accounts that conveyed both manufactured hell and moments of humanity. *If This Is A Man, The Periodic Table of the Elements* and *Moments of Reprieve*, disturbing enough in themselves, were books that found a very remote echo in their reflections on chaos, carnage and reprieve in the destruction and freezing conditions of northern Pakistan, where I first read them.

Somehow the books began to make sense in that context, and the context began to make sense from the books. As things began to settle into some sort of a routine during the response, we would call it a day at around nine in the evening and head off to find what privacy and silence we could in search of solace from the endlessly urgent and competing demands of the day. I had just heard that my university thesis had been accepted for publication and, after staring intently into the glowing radiator bars for half an hour, I would switch on my computer again and start reading and editing my work on Andrey Bely—an obscure, experimental, and somewhat anarchic Russian author. Plot and narrative were dispensed with in his works: characters represented only by their salient features (an ambulant nose, a feather boa) would move in and out of the chapters, while the language itself had been written so as to emulate the ticking of a time bomb that would eventually blow up St Petersburg and with it the ordered and linear streetscape of the rationally organised state. While this had seemed intriguing, if bizarre, when viewed from the British Library where I wrote my thesis, these descriptions strangely seemed to make sense in Pakistan. Cities had literally been destroyed and the fractured, disconnected prose of this experimental novel, which had initially made it almost unreadable, actually began to take on new meaning. In the destruction of the earthquake the rationally organised state was nowhere to be seen, while moments of continuity and recovery carried the absurdity of fleeting encounters whose own salient features remained etched in my mind, such as the orange sellers setting up brightly coloured stalls in the ruined city of Balakot. Such images would continue throughout my career, like the bottles of Coke kept cool in holes in the ground in Darfur.

A week's mandatory rest and recreation, coincidentally in Germany, compounded the sense of alienation in catastrophe. Despite the elegance and solidity of the country's reconstructed cities, every corner of every square seemed to have been annotated with the memorials of crimes past. At one stage, finding a corner of Berlin near the Humboldt University in the (appropriately renamed) Bebelplatz, I stood in the sun and looked for a moment at the attractive view of neoclassical buildings dominating the square. This was an illusory moment of tranquillity, as I soon realised I was standing over a glass paving stone under which stood an empty white bookshelf—the very place where the Nazi regime had burned 'un-German' books more than seventy years earlier. Unable to escape from either the reality or the collective memory of death and destruction, I got on the next train and fled to Belgium—an artificial buffer state between the European powers and itself the product of European conflict: a cartographic attempt to discourage wars between France and Germany. A short stroll the next day down the imposing grandeur of the Avenue des Colonies, built from the profits of King Leopold's peculiarly brutal nineteenth-century occupation of the Congo, immediately put paid to my hope of finding somewhere not contaminated by violence. Thinking, for some reason, that I might find this escape on a tour of the Royal Palace, I soon found myself in the Hall of Mirrors gazing at another massacre: an enormous insect-like chandelier and ceiling decoration constructed from the phosphorescent wings plucked from 1.6 million *Buprestidae* beetles. These were quite common and not an endangered species, according to the information plaque in the hall, but this claim seemed unlikely given the aestheticised scale of this entomological carnage.

I couldn't wait to get back to Pakistan and was not sure what was more disquieting—the monuments to savagery in a European 'dark continent' or the contemporary state of crisis in which I lived. At the very least, while Europe seemed in constant mourning over its appalling wars, in Pakistan, at the time, there was a humanitarian moment caused by the shock of the earthquake—a random calamity rather than the deliberate and genocidal expansionist ambitions of states. Everyone was taken totally by surprise, and there was a brief sense of common purpose to do something urgently, even as calculations of political interest and influence to be gained from the disaster began to brew.

I was redeployed to Muzaffarabad, the destroyed capital of Kashmir and the epicentre of the earthquake, which still hosted the majority of the people living in residual camps. A group of British MPs from the cross-party House of Commons International Development Committee was coming through, and this was seen as an important opportunity to make a strong case for increased aid for the 'second winter' and to add external pressure on the government to allow preparatory relief operations. I was responsible for looking after the MPs and presenting our case.

It was a strange, heartening and baffling experience. I met with the committee's clerk before meeting the MPs themselves and was impressed. She had a PhD in development and had read every report and studied UN maps and was exceptionally well-informed. She took no persuading that we faced a humanitarian crisis, albeit on a smaller scale, unless aid agencies were funded and given authority to act. Elated, and somewhat awed by her clear command of the situation, I drove out to the Muzaffarabad helipad to meet the MPs—a collection of Labour, Conservative and Liberal Democrat representatives who served on one of the most sought-after parliamentary committees. I had instructions to give them twenty minutes at their hotel (a cracked concrete wreck and the only hotel still standing in the town) and to take them straight out to the camps. 'They're not here for a holiday,' I'd been told—'they mean business.'

After a round of vigorous greetings, we piled into a bus and I took the opportunity to rehearse my arguments to the committee clerk as we sat next to each other, before a more formal meeting with the exalted parliamentarians that evening. It was a warm day and brilliant sunlight streamed into the bus. Looking round during a lull in conversation, I saw that all the MPs had fallen asleep, heads lolling in an intercontinental coma of jet lag and sun.

'Where the hell are we?' asked one of the MPs as we stopped outside the first camp—a short, sharp scramble up a rock-strewn path from the road. I tried to explain but he wandered off, returning to the bus unconsoled.

'He thinks his entire constituency in the UK is from here and he's a bit worried about re-election,' the clerk reassured me as I tried to wake up the others. The Labour MPs struggled, and one had to be carried up the hill; the one Conservative was up in an instant, ripping off his shirt and storming up the path. I ran between the two, trying to keep an eye on the Conservative while lending a hand pushing the Labour MPs on. The Liberal Democrats walked at a medium pace, able to manage by themselves but conscious of our efforts to keep everyone together.

'It reminds me of Scotland,' one of them said to me during a breather. 'My constituency would have been like this in the nineteenth century.' He scanned the arid hills, looking over the tents and mud houses that were now coming into view. While some of the community leaders had been informed about our visit, word had clearly not got out to the residents themselves. Catching up with the Conservative, I found him standing in the entrance to one of the tents, interrogating an unsuspecting family in resonant English tones. They looked stunned at the arrival of a semi-clad European.

'What's this all about?' he roared. 'Why are you still here?'

Our translator struggled. 'They don't want to go back,' he said. 'They don't have a house.'

'Looks like a case of aid dependency to me,' replied the Conservative, and shot off disappearing over a hill.

'It must be terrible being disabled,' said one of the Liberal Democrats, staring back down the path we'd just climbed. 'Imagine doing this in a wheelchair.'

The Labour representatives had by now given up and were sitting morosely on a rock halfway up, discussing internecine debates in Oxfam in the eighties about whether the organisation should be 'humanitarian' or a 'development agency'.

Back at the bus, I was becoming worried. The Conservative had failed to reappear, while the MP whose Pakistani-dominated constituency somehow threatened his political career had refused to leave the bus. At last I found the Conservative, standing on a rock looking at the view—shirt on this time, but open to the waist.

'Good job,' he declared, 'nothing to be seen here,' and trotted off back to the bus. He later famously featured in the UK parliamentary expenses scandal in which he had claimed thousands of pounds for the renovation of the bell tower in his eighteenth-century mansion. State assistance for bell towers or moat cleaning was clearly acceptable, but a new tent for someone living in a residual camp facing a freezing winter was not.

Back in Muzaffarabad the winter had started and, as predicted, the camps turned to mud. We had received some funds to work and were now attempting to 'winterise' the leaky canvas from the year before, wrapping tents in huge quantities of plastic, digging drainage ditches and trying to ensure that they were nowhere the camp toilets, whose effluent drained randomly. The rains increased and the ground became increasingly waterlogged.

The Refugee Commissioner had continued to try to pull down the camps where he could and send people 'home', back up the windy, unstable roads whose edges had been deeply corroded by the earthquake and had fallen into the deep Himalayan ravines and valleys below. I joined up with a specialist 'alpine unit' from the UN Operations Department to monitor return conditions in winter of a convoy of thirty vehicles heading from Muzaffarabad to the Leepa Valley. The report was stark:

```
At an altitude of 2700 metres, a new snow ava-
lanche had descended and blocked the road. The
avalanche had been partially cleared but posed a
significant obstacle to vehicles, being at a steep
incline and on a tight hairpin bend. It took a
skilled local driver in a jeep 20 minutes to tra-
verse the avalanche debris. There was a further
sector of the road where avalanches were expected.
It was observed that, further on, deep mud ruts
were developing on the road surface. By 16h00 the
weather began to deteriorate with a cold north
wind and freezing rain falling. By 16h20 a group
of 8 jeeps were blocked by a snow avalanche. The
drivers did not appear to be skilled in these con-
ditions and their attempts to pass were weak and
disorganised. None of the vehicles had snow chains
and the tyres were worn and lacked deep tread. A
second wave of 12 vehicles arrived at 17h20. Dark-
ness due to fall at 17h40.
```

With further snow expected at higher altitudes, return by road was, in the words of the alpine team, 'a dubious policy in safety terms'. We discussed alternatives if the road was inaccessible—there was some spare helicopter capacity, and if the people and the government agreed there was a possibility of flying the camp's residents back to their places of origin in the Leepa Valley, but we had to be sure that life and livelihoods were sustainable when they got there, and this was dubious given what we knew about the road at the relatively low attitude of 2700 metres. The best thing was for people to remain in the camp with as many relief supplies and as much 'winterisation' as we could get. But when I got back to the camp the next day they had disappeared—driven out by more government trucks, along the extremely hazardous road to their destroyed homes that were now under snow.

Outraged at our inability to get any sort of reasonable solution to the problem of residual camps, I contacted two journalists from the BBC and they agreed to head up and film the results. If we could get nowhere through negotiation, then our last resort was to expose what was happening. But by now the route was untraceable and the people who had been in the camp had disappeared into the mountains. The BBC crew filmed miserable snow-clad villages and the nerve-wracking jeep manoeuvres past avalanches on unstable roads. The film ended with an interview over tea with the commissioner's wife. 'The relief effort is going very well,' she said. 'Its simply swimmingly marvellous.'

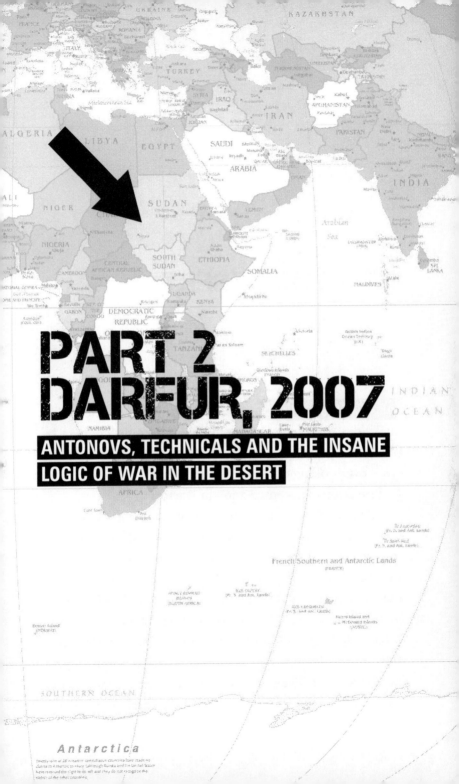

PART 2
DARFUR, 2007

ANTONOVS, TECHNICALS AND THE INSANE
LOGIC OF WAR IN THE DESERT

CHAPTER 7
INTO THE DESERT

CALLING FROM THE TOP of a rubbish dump in the earth-quake-destroyed city in Muzaffarabad, I could connect by phone to Khartoum. And from the foothills of the Himalayas, overlooking the Vale of Kashmir and the Neelum and Jhelum rivers, I accepted a job in Darfur.

'Time to move,' I was told by wiser heads. 'Once the emergency phase is over the politics starts, development intervenes, and nothing happens.' During the earthquake, the mantra of relief workers was 'Don't make a catastrophe out of a crisis'. The real catastrophe was elsewhere—no matter how bad the destruction and loss of life in Pakistan, it was a different order of magnitude to the catastrophe of Darfur. All disasters and emergencies are to some degree 'man-made': in Pakistan, we saw complicity through poor construction standards and a sluggish government response.

In Darfur the decision had been taken by the country's president and senior leaders to kill, rape and displace, systematically and indiscriminately, whole groups of people based on an increasingly racialised conception of ethnicity. Belatedly, and after the worst of the killing spree was over, the international community had turned its head towards Darfur.

From Islamabad I flew to Melbourne, wincing as the customs officer in Lahore stamped my passport with a red X and the words *Do not readmit*, and from Melbourne to London and then back again across the globe to Dubai, and Amman and Khartoum. I sat next to young Americans mostly on this Middle Eastern leg—some naive and some sceptical, the fresh-faced and the haggard, mercenaries and Wilsonian internationalists. It was my reading matter that started the conversations on the plane—and ironic, perhaps, that Orwell had become hallowed ground for these illiberal interventionists going to reshape the Middle East.

I flew on, transcending worlds and time while watching videos in my metal tube, until fifty hours after I started, dots of houses emerged from the expanse of desert tan, clinging tightly to the confluence of the White and Blue Niles. From the air Khartoum came into view—not the resonant place of my imagination conjured by the words *Omdurman* and *dervish*, the place of heroic imperial last stands, the literal and metaphorical 'heart of Africa'—but a neat, modern city arranged in lines, perched precariously on the edge of vast waves of desert tending massively and irrevocably to the interior.

'Call me Ernie,' he said. 'My name's Hernando, but all the guys in Geneva call me Ernie—do you know the guys in Geneva?'

I regretted that I didn't know the guys in Geneva, and it was a refrain that echoed again and again as my newly arrived colleague Ernie and I made our way from the hotel to the Khartoum office and back again. We had both been sent to the 'operation' in Sudan, knew no one, and had little conception of what we were actually supposed to do. After a brief meeting with my supervisor, whose only words—'I see you've made it'—were uttered without looking up between emails, I remained unenlightened.

'Don't worry,' Ernie reassured me when I wondered how long we were going to sit around in Khartoum, 'the guys in Geneva are all over it.'

But the days passed slowly as I went through endless rounds of briefings. A political advisor from the UN took me into the organisation's map room, where I stood gazing at the neat, sanitised cartography of war. Maps of flat, empty space marked with crosses to indicate major battles, circles for cities, and triangles to show refugee camps. Dotted lines marked possible roads whose existence and accessibility no one could really guarantee. The only permanent fixtures were thick black lines representing international borders, labelled *Libya* and *Chad*—a misplaced assertion of certainty, as I discovered, because these borders meant nothing in a conflict that engulfed the Sahara, a conflict that found its geographical echo in drought, displacement and gradual desertification. The movements of time, politics and a changing climate had little use for lines on maps. Layered onto these humanitarian maps was a political map that showed spreading, amorphous shapes that represented estimates of areas under the control of a dozen pro-government and rebel groups—expanding, contracting, realigning with the cruel exigencies of irregular desert warfare. 'Nobody really knows what they represent,' said the political advisor. 'It's the best we can do but most of it's made up in Khartoum.'

As I was going into the 'field', I was subjected to a comprehensive security briefing. I was told how to walk around a car before getting in and what to do if a lion suddenly appeared. There had been a vast and unexpected migration of animals across the continent that year and I was to stay clear of marauding gazelle. Snakes were generally considered bad, and the gung-ho security advisor discussed the relative merits of 'going it' if attacked by gunmen on a motorbike while driving. Clearly living in a world of action movies, he thought the best approach would be to ram them. He had never actually been out of Khartoum, he confided. The SAS motto *Who dares, wins* was clearly an inspiration to him, although he'd had to adapt it for civilian humanitarian workers. As he sent me on my way he slapped me on the back, saying, 'Who lives, wins!'

Sudan appeared further and further away. Ernie had managed to find himself a filing cabinet and a desk, where he spent his days furiously busy with reams of paperwork. Our newbie camaraderie diminished to a tight-lipped grunt over coffee in the morning at the hotel. Lunchtime walks revealed empty, quiet streets, and aside from the fine clinging dust on my boots, I found nothing beyond an elegant pizza restaurant with a garden setting and a French-speaking chef. There were shops and supermarkets; an international embargo meant that even though the banking system did not operate, the shelves were overflowing with imported produce, priced in US dollars. In the centre of town, a curved plate-glass tower modelled on London's Gherkin had just been finished, shunning both gravity and right-angles in its ultra-modernity.

After work I was taken by colleagues to a cafe by the Nile. Surrounded by lush ferns we sat outside with Khartoum's elite, watching the sunset in the thick, humid heat of the early evening, cooled by water vapour sprayed across the garden, and ate freshly made sorbet. 'This is the most peaceful city in the world. There is no crime here,' someone said without a trace of irony.

And yet everything around was evidence of massive state-sponsored criminality. The wealth of Khartoum and the immense prosperity of its sorbet-sucking residents were the product of decades of economic, political and cultural strangulation of the rest of the country by Sudan's riverine elite. Shortly before I arrived, the International Criminal Court had issued arrest warrants for senior cabinet ministers, including the head of the Orwellian Humanitarian Aid Commission, for genocide and crimes against humanity in Darfur. This was a prelude to the ICC's subsequent indictment of the country's head of state, Omar al-Bashir, for the same crimes, authorised by him but carried out by radicalised local militias called *janjawiid* (a compound word derived from the G3 rifle, *jawad* meaning horse and an Eastern Sudanese dialect word for outlaws). These turbaned 'devils on horseback' had contributed to the deaths of between 350,000 and 450,000 people, with another 3.5 million—more than half of Darfur's population—displaced and in need of humanitarian assistance. 'You are informed', wrote *janjawiid* leader Musa Hilal to one of his subordinates in Darfur, citing orders from President Bashir himself, 'that directives have been issued … to change the demography of Darfur and empty it of its African tribes'.[1] It was becoming clear that the 'guys in Geneva' really didn't have a clue.

As we flew over El Fasher airport in North Darfur in a Cessna C-130 on a UN Humanitarian Air Service flight, the military realities of the maps I'd studied earlier in Khartoum—with their lines, legends and amorphous colouring of the political landscape—began to dawn. On the edge of the runway, new helicopter gunships sat ready for action, but were dwarfed by an enormous white plane.

'That's the Antonov,' the South African pilot muttered as we landed, and I made my way past bored guards and towards a small shop selling gleaming lines of cold Pepsi.

The Antonov was the white elephant of the war in Darfur: vast, lumbering, and symbolic of the regime's indiscriminate killing. It was a Soviet-era military cargo plane designed to carry tanks, but in Darfur it was used as an instrument of terror. It flew over villages dropping bombs that were rolled out from its giant hold by hand—killing that was at once industrial and primitive. The Antonov was painted white—the colour of humanitarian agencies—and before I arrived its wings had been marked with the letters *UN*, showing the regime's total disregard for life, law and the work of aid organisations. Each evening at dusk, from the concrete room where we worked, all conversation was

---

[1] quoted in J Flint & A de Waal, *Darfur: A New History of a Long War*, Zed Books, London, 2008.

drowned in the roar of its engines as the Antonov took off for another bombing run from the same airstrip used to bring in humanitarian workers and supplies.

The Antonov instilled terror and targeted not rebel combatants but clusters of villages, food stores and water wells, but the truly deadly assaults came from militias armed with 'technicals'. In the early days of the conflict the militias had been mounted on horseback or camels, but as the war progressed Khartoum armed them with technicals— Land Cruisers with the top sawn off and mounted with a machine gun. They were used with the Antonov in coordinated attacks on civilians. These attacks were aimed not only at wiping out people but their means of subsistence as well—'to change the demography', as Musa Hilal had put it. 'They kill us because of our black faces,' said one man I spoke to months later in a village called Doruk that had been attacked.

For three weeks before the mission, I listened to the sounds of war, closed up in concrete offices, protected by floodlights, barbed wire and the flags, colours and protective heraldry of the international community. Curfew at seven, radio check at ten—*This is Foxtrot Mike loud and clear.* At six each evening, as I finished work at the office, all thoughts and conversations were drowned by the raw noise and aggression of the Antonov taking off for its evening bombing run.

During the day, I inhabited a small, hot, concrete bunker with blocked-in windows. From this makeshift office I worked as a 'protection officer', trying to gather information about population movements and the humanitarian conditions of people displaced by the Darfur conflict. Going home one evening through a back street near the market, I turned suddenly onto the main road and pulled up sharp as a technical accelerated past. Camouflage, rocket launchers, guns, and the shouts of men moving out of town, seeking a kill. A roar of noise went up—a full-blooded bark simultaneously bursting from twenty men on edge—as the mounted machine gun slowly turned towards the car. And in the car's cabin, paralysis took hold and my brain went numb; my white and useless strapped-in limbs drooped heavily into the seat. A distorted voice—my own—wrenched in through the din with instructions for every muscle and every action. *Move slowly, put your hand on the gears, put the car in reverse, move slowly, drive back, go slow, get back, shrink away, retreat.* And as they receded, the sweat came, the shaking and the nausea.

At dusk, the firing started from outside town. In our compound, recently equipped with satellite TV, men watched Milan Fashion Week to the irregular detonations from the firing range until it was time for the insurgency channel—amateur videos of militia violence filmed in Iraq, watched by aid workers in Darfur. Parallel realities that only intersected on one occasion when a stray bullet that had been fired into the air smashed through the roof and embedded itself in the concrete floor of the TV room.

Despite the sounds around us, Darfur was remote. We were locked away in offices and compounds, barely allowed out because of the passing traffic of militia and the endless fluctuations of alliances between local commanders and factions—Sudan rarely imposed. The billowing dust from a sweeper's broom in the morning, the rich Arabic coffee in the afternoon, took me temporarily away from maps, computer screens and reports of fighting, casualties, people on the move.

'They're trying to fuck us over,' my boss would say each morning, but she was referring to our colleagues in Khartoum.

I was involved in two major field 'missions', as humanitarian operations were called, in a language that merged military with missionary terminology. These involved organising refugee convoys from conflict-affected areas on the Chad–West Darfur border and leading assessment teams in search of recently displaced people in North Darfur in an area called Dar Zaghawa. Initially, the intent had been to monitor the humanitarian conditions of people returning to their places of origin following the signing of the Darfur Peace Agreement (DPA) in 2006. This peace was ineffective, however, and was ignored by all sides. It had further split Darfurian opposition groups, making successive peace negotiations more difficult, and had provided an inadequate basis for an African Union intervention force that lacked the resources, mandate and military cohesion to alter the course of the war. Despite initial high hopes, it had been mired in bureaucracy and could not even provide effective protection to women collecting water in camps—a daily task that took women outside the nominal security of the camps' perimeter and brought with it the risk of rape, murder and abduction—let alone for the dispersed rural civilian population in an area the size of France. As a result of its failings, the African Union force had become so detested that Darfuri rebel groups had started to attack it. Some weeks after I arrived, fifteen Senegalese soldiers were killed in a raid led by the one Darfuri rebel organisation that had actually signed the DPA and had earlier supported the establishment of a peacekeeping mission. It was, as one military observer noted, 'classic peacekeeping in an environment so wildly not a classic peace as to be ridiculous'. For the people of Darfur, there had been no peace and no one was going home. In a war frequently referred to as 'our Spain', the efforts to end a mass crime that toxically fused a racialised state ideology with brutal power calculations lacked international resources, commitment, and sincerity.

What was happening in Darfur was new and represented a vicious unravelling of the old order. In the 1980s, the academic Alex de Waal had travelled to Darfur and met with a leading tribal elder called Sheikh Hilal Musa, father of the notorious militia leader Musa Hilal. In a tent sparsely furnished with saddles, carpets, water jars and spears—the possessions of a life of desert nomadism—the old sheikh had recounted a 'moral geography' of the land. This was a grid, drawn in the sand, which showed an interlocking pattern of land use and migration. Nomads and camel herders had travelled along transhumance routes that occupied certain squares on the grid, while agriculturalists occupied others. When the nomads moved into an area they tended it well, looked after gardens, protected villages and left it safe to return. Similarly, agriculturalists allowed access to grazing lands as the herders moved from pasture to pasture with the changing seasons. Gifts were exchanged—on arrival a goat would be sacrificed for the herders by the agriculturalists, and on their departure a camel would be given to the agriculturalists in return. The linguistic, religious and ethnic make-up of Darfur reflected this cooperation. An independent sultanate until 1916, when it was annexed to the Anglo-Egyptian Sudan, Darfur had developed its own separate social fabric and state identity. Arabic had become the common language, in addition to the local tribal languages, and intermarriage was common—making the region almost uniquely cosmopolitan. There was a strong tradition of Sufi Islam, which synchretised Muslim and local traditions of religious practice. 'African' and 'Arab' were not meaningful divisions in Darfur and even Sheikh Hilal, despite his casual racism and assumptions of the superiority of his tribe and nomadic way of life, boasted about his 'African' antecedents.

By the 1980s, however, his world had ended. Drought, desertification and famine had disrupted the earlier moral geography, and as the great camel herds began to die off from a lack of grazing land, nomads came into conflict with agriculturalists while searching for new pastures. In some cases they attempted to abandon their herds and started to farm as an alternative livelihood, but this met with resistance from already settled populations. Nomadic tribes that would later be identified as 'Arab' and associated with the *janjawiid* were, at the outset, also victims.

While conflict mounted internally, exacerbated in part by a changing climate, Darfur was caught in the middle of the geopolitics of Khartoum, Tripoli and N'Djamena. In Khartoum, increasingly Islamist governments took office. A military coup brought Omar al-Bashir to power in 1989 and the regime increasingly defined itself in opposition to the predominantly Christian and animist South, in an ongoing war that left more than two million dead, and promoted a strict adherence to a racialised conception of Islam. At the same time Libya's dictator, Colonel Gaddafi, embarked on the creation of an 'Arab belt' across the Sahara. Central to this geopolitical project was control of Chad. Darfur, which borders both countries, was used as a base by Libyan-backed Chadian militias fighting against the government in the capital N'Djamena. Gaddafi sponsored the establishment of the Islamic Legion, consisting of Chadian rebels and discontented Sahelian Arabs, who were displaced from their lands and livelihoods by drought and local conflict. The Islamic Legion was trained by the Libyan regime in a toxic mix of desert guerilla warfare and a virulent form of Arab supremacism. The defeat of the Islamic Legion in 1988 had a profound impact as its fighters returned to Darfur and formed the Arab Gathering—an armed political movement ostensibly organised to protect the interests of a disadvantaged minority within Sudan, but possessed of weapons, training and an ideology of racial supremacy.

As an 'Arab' identity was being cultivated by extremist movements in Tripoli and Khartoum, an 'African' identity was also being manufactured. The resistance leader of South Sudan, John Garang, sought to alter the course of the North–South war by enlisting non-Arab tribes (who were a majority of the overall population of Sudan) to a common cause with the South, whose sub-Saharan identity and predominantly Christian religion were more easily identified as 'African'. This initially had little traction in Darfur, as the early stages of Khartoum's Islamist turn promised to include all good Muslims—defined by conformity with increasingly strict religious practice rather than by race—in the affairs and rewards of the state.

By 2000, however, it appeared that this offer was a sham.

When Bashir took power in 1989, he replaced this inclusive version of Islam with one that emphasised the primacy of his own and Khartoum's Arabised elite. The regime in Khartoum did not invest its resources in Darfur as had been promised and the Darfurian opposition produced a 'Black Book' that documented this systematic political and economic neglect along racial lines. In this context, John Garang's offer of 'African' or 'non-Arab' solidarity took on greater political appeal. In 2003, two Darfuri opposition groups—the Sudanese Liberation Army (SLA) and the Justice and Equality Movement (JEM)—united and attacked a government base in El Fasher to instigate armed opposition to the regime in Khartoum. Already massively in debt and fully committed to the war with South Sudan, Bashir responded to this new threat by exploiting Darfur's already ideologically radicalised and alienated groups to create ruthless local militias prepared to kill for money and land: the *janjawiid*. This was, Alex de Waal has written, 'counter-insurgency on the cheap' and represented a radically different, nightmare world from that in which the eighty-year old Sheikh Hilal had grown up and in which his son, Musa Hilal, was to become one of the most vicious protagonists.[2]

My field notes from this time recorded, in terse shorthand form, this radicalisation of the war in Darfur and reflected a complex society that had collapsed from both external and internal pressure. As we travelled further and further into Darfur, passing burned out villages and interviewing

[2] A de Waal, 'Counter-insurgency on the cheap', *London Review of Books* 26 (15), August 2004.

people hiding in dry wadis (seasonal rivers) or around clumps of trees, fearing attack from the passing Antonov, my notes became increasingly cryptic. In handwriting shaky from the road, smudged with dust and sweat, a grim record of people's marginal survival was scratched into the page. An 'X' in every village indicted the last attack, while number and downward arrows indicated the levels of population decline. This survey of living conditions ceased to reflect any individuality of person or location and assumed instead an almost bland sameness that emerged from the shorthand of destruction:

Last X 3 months ago. No food, some berries. Water 6hrs by donkey. Living in forest, animals stolen. Families separated. Majority killed in X. Currently living in Wadi. Water holes bombed/pumps destroyed. Ongoing JJ [janjawiid] attacks. Primary/Secondary displacement. Push factors. Antonov seen yesterday at 4pm—live in constant expectation of attack.

- *Shardaba*

- *Songoli*

- *Gurbuhir*

- *Sonjabak .... Empty/destroyed*

- *Argao*

- *Urubukir*

GoS [Government of Sudan] harassment—women at risk when collecting water. Seven women from this village have disappeared. Access to water 6 hours by donkey. In nearby Ana

Bagi, 4 girls had recently disappeared because of attacks by the GoS forces.

Orschi—attack on school 3 months ago also problem of being near the main road which is controlled by GoS and JJ—animals looted and now no access to markets. Living in forests on seeds and berries and staple millet They might eat meat every 2-3 months, but have given us one of their goats for dinner. In Inni, there are attacks every week. Last week the JJ took 62 cows and 5 camels. JJ kill/loot.

Gita—Evidence of malnutrition—no agriculture, no animals. Former land now a JJ base and the village and families have become separated and many still lost.

Hilalia. The Antonov attacked one week ago, and people are now living in the forest. They had been in camps in Chad but were also attacked here on a weekly basis by Chadian rebels and the camp itself was located in an unstable area with little water. They are safer here than in the camp although things are clearly difficult. The water well was bombed and daily water collection takes 5 hours by donkey—a task that is done by the women. The SLA control the area so, currently, this is relatively safe. But—there is a nearby GoS position and one week ago a village woman was kidnapped and raped. There was SLA 'retribution' and 'an exchange' between GoS and the SLA at the water point. The wells, however, are only full during the rainy season and dry up during the summer. Food is also scarce and the villagers are dependent on food from camps in Chad where some are still registered or through extended family/tribal connections—5 days away by donkey. Food collection is also a women's task.

Haramumba—fearing constant attacks water is collected at night.

Ana Bagi—located near GoS checkpoint on a hill: a constant threat. There was a rape ten days ago.

As Darfur fades from the headlines, overshadowed by the independence of South Sudan, and official assertions from the US, the UK and the UN that the situation has 'stabilised', the destruction of this starkly beautiful desert society continues. While the killing and displacement reached their peak in 2004 and have declined since, the Antonov still flies. The situation is perhaps more complex as, in addition to state-sponsored violence, the Darfuri rebel groups have begun to turn on each other and unity is further away than ever. But Darfur remains a marginalised part of North Sudan—still governed by a military elite and underpinned by a profoundly racist ideology. Despite ICC indictments Bashir remains in charge, uncensured by other African leaders and in control in a capital still booming from oil revenues. Aid agencies remain on the ground providing vital supplies for the nearly four million people who have been displaced, but this task is routinely made almost impossible by the regime's total lack of cooperation and is still overseen by the ICC-indicted Humanitarian Aid Commission. Peace for Darfuris—as for other minorities within this ideologised rump state of North Sudan—remains as elusive as ever. And what has been lost, apart from hundreds of thousands of lives, is a society whose fusion of Arab and African cultures representing East and West, Saharan and sub-Saharan, animist and Muslim, may well be impossible to restore. As another old sheikh lamented, a few days from his own eightieth birthday:

> *The Arabs came here looking for pasture, and when the grass was finished they went back. They used up our grass, but they took good care of the gardens and the people. There were no robberies, no thieves, no revolution. No one thought of domination, everyone was safe … Now there is nothing but trouble all over Sudan. There is no government, no control. Look around you. What do you see? No women, only armed men. We no longer recognize it, this land of ours.* [3]

For Orwell, history notionally ended in the 1930s with the defeat of Republican Spain. Seventy years later, a history of pluralism and relatively peaceful accommodation has ended in Darfur in a parallel world of extremist ideologies and the inhuman calculus of political power.

[3] Sheikh Heri Rahma quoted in J Flint & A de Waal, *Darfur: A New History of a Long War*, Zed Books, London, 2008, p. 276.

CHAPTER 8
THE MISSION

IT IS STRANGE, the rituals that we find ourselves carrying out before the unknown—detached acts, learned by rote, and made solemn by the occasion. I shaved not once but three times, showered twice, arranged my books first by content, then by colour, then by size. I put on the cleanest of clean clothes—a red shirt, blue trousers, grey desert boots—and stepped out of my dark concrete room onto the street and into the dust of El Fasher.

Outside our compound we were engaged in silent activity, making final preparations for the mission. Conversation was pared back to what was strictly necessary—all the more lucid and eloquent for its truncated, listlike form: ballistics blanket, full medical kit, small medical kit, run bag, 180 litres of petrol, camp beds, water, food, fire extinguishers, sat phone, HF radio, VHF radio, radio call-sign list, travel authorisation, GPS, white and blue flags. Body bags were stored under the back seat of the Toyota Land Cruiser Troop Carrier—a large and highly prized car known throughout Darfur for its speed, agility and long desert range. A car used by aid workers and coveted by killers. Take off the roof, attach a machine gun and you have a 'technical'—a makeshift instrument of war capable of striking deep into the continent. We called it the Buffalo, and with its dual fuel tanks, power and relatively light weight, it could cover 1000 kilometres without refuelling. With this car, the chance of attack and hijacking increased, and we had four of them and 100 kilometres of sand, scrub and stone before us—a lawless area known as the Janjaweed Damra. The instructions were simple in this flat no man's land whose aridity was starkly etched in dried-up water courses and burnt-out villages. *Drive as fast as you can.*

That, and our rituals. All glowed and squeaked with cleanliness. Beards were neatly trimmed, white robes shone against the sand and sky, the cars were freshly polished and the light-blue flags of the United Nations flew high. Each bound tight around his arm Koranic inscriptions impressed on leather pouches. Allah, the merciful, the compassionate—keep away the bullets.

The night before, in a small coffee shop, the mission's leadership—the security officer, the logistics officer and I—made our final preparations. Everything had been done, the cars stocked and fuelled, fuel dumps prearranged. We had hundreds of forms: forms for assessment, forms for recording, forms for observing. All the bureaucracy for inscribing the needs and living conditions of people living in fear, scared of attack, on the move. Administration for the displaced. I thought I had trained for this, 'skilled-up', prepared. In Pakistan I had seen living cities reduced to knee-high rubble; frontier lands where peasant farmers in mud-brick villages were attacked by soldiers of the state, their lands laid waste. Darfur was our responsibility, our Spain. And so we sat in the coffee hut and spoke and in our final preparation raised the questions only our rituals could answer.

We started, a convoy of white and blue weaving like tracers through the desert. We maintained a tight line of sight and constant radio contact, fanning out to avoid the blinding dust of the car in front. There was a strict protocol where the most important positions were the lead and the tail, a defensive formation to protect the cars in between. Together, in convoy, watching. We communicated in terse radio form, constantly checking and rechecking our positions: *Mobile Four, Mobile One—are you with us, over.* Behind us came the vehicle belonging to a lone NGO—outside the UN security arrangements, behind the convoy. Before we left I went for a final security briefing. 'They go for the last car,' I had been told. 'If anything happens, don't stop. They're nice guys, but they're not your responsibility.'

But they were—the colour of our flags conferred status, an implication of government, a suggestion of international authority. In the lead car, my white skin had ceased to be my own and, like the flags above, had been lent to the mission as a guarantee of safety.

I was in the lead and I was the least knowledgeable about this land. When I had flown over it in the Cessna it had seemed to me to be a landscape of unparalleled bleakness. I had spent the last two years among the soft colours, streams and tucked-away hamlets of Pakistan's mountainous north. Sudan was a murderous counterpoint. In that desert, I could not survive. I could not read the land or determine a path. My electronic compass simply showed empty space intersected 1000 kilometres to the north by a straight line and the word *Libya*. My notebooks were a list of twelve-digit map coordinates, measuring degrees, feet and inches east and north, no names or places. Before I left I had seen a political map of Darfur—amorphous colours shifting and blending into one another as alliances broke down, opposition movements split, and government favourites charted their own course. The open skies and desert space were strangely and intensely claustrophobic and as we drove, my eyes strained, searching the country for checkpoints and militia factions.

And soon enough, we saw the checkpoint—in the distance a little nest of rocket launchers poked over half a dozen sandbags in the sun. I had not seen it, there were no markings, but it commanded the track and marked a random pocket of political control in the sand. Black soldiers from the South, bought and brought by Khartoum, armed by Russia, funded by Chinese oil investments to man an outpost in Darfur. Soldiers of the Government of Sudan.

At speed we continued, and amid the churning dust we passed deserted hut after deserted hut where the remains of villages had been left gradually to collapse. I saw the black, charred outline of houses burned indelibly into the ground. I shouted at the driver after some subterranean feud over precedence caused him to clip the tail of the car in front—the surrounding desolation slowly eating its way into our small party. Here, I was told, was the school for boys—a roofless, bullet-ridden building of handmade brick. There, was the girls' school—an inferior wooden structure marked by nothing now except a few small pieces of charcoal.

In the storm that engulfed us, stinging our eyes and choking us, we walked through an abandoned town where shot-up schools, abandoned shops and bombed wells loomed out of the grey, stinging particles. Near the border of Chad, a child came up to me holding his head and said the single word '*malade*' before disappearing again into the dust.

Camels and goats gathered round a waterhole, tended by women in vibrant reds and yellows to the sound of a water pump's constant grind and hammer. Near our car a man, slightly older than the rest, laughed insanely and struck poses with a Kalashnikov and a makeshift wooden cross-brace, egged on by the men in search of entertainment after a long drive. Eyes wide, hair wild in matted dreadlocks, grinning, aiming, firing—the sound of imitation gunshots rasping from his distended throat. I took away the cameras and disbursed the teams to get them away from this pitiful, derelict sight. Our rebel escort looked on impassively from their battered camouflage technical, the turbaned commander the only adult among them, aside from the driver. A fourteen-year-old stood listlessly holding a rocket launcher and watched with expressionless eyes as the old man re-fought a war with invisible weapons and an invisible enemy in front of him.

I walked away from the cars and away from the waterhole—the dinning of the pump slowly fading away, the small huts becoming swallowed up in the dust and the uniformly dun-coloured horizon. And on I walked, striding now to get away form the others, almost at a run, so good to use my limbs again after being in the car, away from engines, the crackle of radio contact, the bucking and lurching of the Buffalo as it careened over ruts and ridges in the sand. Behind me was the escort commander, unarmed this time, barefoot in camouflage uniform, and the village elders in white gowns and turbans carrying the walking sticks that marked their high office. On we walked, fast, deliberate, purposeful, away from the village to the forest where the people now lived.

Once again I led but was blind to the surrounds, absorbed in walking, swinging limbs, clearing my head from the perpetual din and fear. I felt relieved to be outside, away from the others, on my own, moving faster and keeping a slight distance in front of the elders and the commander. A sense of purpose had returned after the jarring chase of the cars. But I missed what we were there to see. At a sharp call from behind me, I turned into a thinly shaded forest and saw for the first time houses buried deep inside—camouflaged, all but invisible.

Here was almost a scene of normality: children played under the watchful eye of their mothers, preparations were beginning for evening meals, fires were being stoked, wood collected. There were no young men—they were away, fighting, moving in a perpetual arc from refugee camps where they were registered and could collect food and organise themselves politically, to their farmland, which they sought to defend, and to their families in hiding in the forest. The houses were made of interlaced branches and

thatched roofs built around the base of the tree trunk—
barely visible from the ground and completely invisible
from the air.

'We came here because of the Antonov,' they said. 'Here
we are safe, they cannot see us in the forest.'

They had been driven there a year ago. The Antonov
had bombed the town and a subsequent land assault by
government-sponsored militia had pushed them back,
the rebels fighting for the land. Periodically the Antonov
returned but there had not been any further land attacks.
The defence had not saved the houses but had saved most
of the people—already, cowering from the air raid, they
heard the land attack revving before dawn.

'I am just a farmer,' an old man told me and reached
down quickly, hands trembling, for a cigarette.

And they were not alone. In town after town the same
stories of displacement and dislocation were repeated. The
mere sound of the Antonov was enough to send people
fleeing for the trees and the wadis. Sometimes it just flew
over, sometimes bombs would fall, sometimes it was the fatal
foreplay for a dawn assault of technicals. Outside another
village, I came across a small group of men sitting under a
tree. There were about twenty of them and the silence was
uncanny. No, they were not from the local village, but they
had taken refuge there—under the tree—and had brought
some of their animals following a surprise attack only two
days before. In the insane calculus of desperation and
destruction some of the men had taken as many animals
as they could—the income and livelihood of the tribe.
They had left women, children and the elderly to find what
sanctuary they could in the care of other members of the

tribe. But now, having escaped, they feared the worst—that those left behind had been caught in the suddenness of the attack, butchered or raped. As we talked, the temperature rose and the exhausted listlessness was replaced quickly with increasing anger and agitation as the men began to find voice and rage. They were now sleeping rough on the outskirts of the village and knew nothing of what had happened to their families or where they were, but thought that the *janjawiid* militia might follow them into Dar Zaghawa, even though they suspected that the majority had been killed in the attacks. One man—tall, dark-skinned, and dressed with an extraordinary dignity—came to me with a book. Abdul Aziz Adum Haroon, the village teacher, had written down all the names of the people in the village before the attack, and had the foresight to take the book with him as he fled. There were 6200 names.

In this atmosphere of fetid hopelessness we worked. And as we talked, stories began to emerge. We came with nothing but our forms to guide us in recording the conditions in which they lived, and told them that we could not deliver or promise anything. We needed information—who, where and what. But nobody seemed to mind; in many ways just our being there mattered—a presence from the outside, a sign of interest and concern, however small and insignificant. For many, simply telling their story was important in itself. Some people told us about their daily routines—the quests for water, food, the bitter taste of ground berries. On more than one occasion, I was taken aside and shown the scars of previous attacks: bullet markings, knife cuts. 'This is what they did—and this'. But always there was the deafening silence of the dead—the subtext of every conversation, the unstated absence in every village, stories present but untold. The only real grief I saw was for a survivor: an elderly man, now largely blind and physically weak, saying farewell to his daughters who had made the decision to send him to a refugee camp, where he might have some hope of food and care. In that village near the Chad border they could barely feed themselves, let alone those who had become dependent, and Darfur is not a place where people grow old. The children here had discoloured hair and enlarged stomachs and they were strangely passive, not moving as the flies settled in numbers around their eyes.

Some had decided to move to the camp, others made the calculation that they would risk staying behind—perhaps to be closer to land, farms or family. To all of us watching it was obvious that, alone and old, the man would not last long. I stood aside, held our convoy, and waited for this last horrendous farewell.

But there were moments of magic too. I laid out a reed matt on the ground each evening and slept outside. One night, unable to sleep, I climbed over the pile of protective sandbags that was our nominal defence, and took the most miraculous night-time stroll of my life, following a moonlit path across a wadi and into Chad. It is the night sky I remember most. I had first become captivated by this in Pakistan where, when work finally finished for the night, I would go out into the winter cold and look up to see the small rust-coloured dot of far-distant Mars—fittingly alien amid the profound disturbance of the earthquake zone where I was working. In Darfur's desert—seen from space, nothing more than a vast tract of darkness—it became possible to look forward to the pyrotechnic brilliance of the night sky. At a certain point after dinner, conversation would stop and people would lie on the ground gazing upwards, transported for the night, away from the sun, the heat and the political realities of the day.

We were generally well looked after by the SLA. They accompanied us on all the roads with their battered technicals and teenage soldiers. They dressed themselves in camouflage turbans with arms tightly bound with numerous *hijab*—small leather pouches containing Koranic verses. Rocket-propelled grenades were strapped to the sides and bonnet of the cars.

The African Union also had a small presence where we stayed in the deserted town called Um Baru. Here, French-speaking Senegalese troops were commanded by a fat Libyan with a large lapel badge showing Colonel Gaddafi waving to a crowd (it was rumoured that when you turned the badge upside down you got a hologram of Hawaiian dancing girls). However, while the colonel and our SLA escort sipped tea and chatted cordially, this relationship was deeply strained. Only a week before, the SLA had attacked the African Union and killed five Senegalese soldiers. Now they were blocking African Union access to the waterhole in murderous protest against the ineffectiveness of this force in stopping the war.

Fearing attacks on the African Union compound, we stayed instead with the SLA, who provided us with a 'guesthouse', a term that proved somewhat misleading. There was a small concrete bunker with disturbing graffiti scratched into the walls by deranged SLA soldiers. It showed technicals and roughly drawn human outlines shooting fire-balls at each other. The other facility was a slaughter area which featured a small tree where a goat (that evening's meal) would be tethered among the carcasses of its caprine cousins.

Out of SLA territory, however, we had less luck. Our car broke down and a driver decided to embark on amateur mechanics. This turned into brake surgery and he eventually discovered that he could not get the dismantled parts back together. After five hours of his banging and cursing, we realised that we could not make it through the next GoS checkpoint and into the nearest town before nightfall. The checkpoints are nothing more than soldiers dug defensively behind rock or on top of a hill commanding the road. These are sensitive areas and have to be approached carefully—the soldiers are undisciplined. They resemble a militia more than a regular army and are often hard to see. After dark, they have orders to shoot on sight. We managed to tow the car back 10 kilometres to the previous checkpoint and spoke to the commander, who reluctantly allowed us to camp in a wadi under the GoS command post on a neighbouring hill. It was an uneasy night—we circled our four cars (one with a defunct back wheel, another with a severely bent front axle) and could not light a fire, cook, or turn on our torches for fear of being shot at. The sand was soft and warm and the night sky brilliant, but at the change of the guard the new commander took a dislike to us and at 5am sent a dozen men with rocket launchers to move us on.

The strain of the previous night then began to turn into farce. We managed to get our car to the next checkpoint (breaking two steel towropes) and rather uneasily left it there, all fourteen people and one sheep piling into the two remaining operable vehicles and limping along as fast as the bent axle would take us. After several overcrowded and dehydrated hours we reached the town of Kutum—the nearest big town with international agencies and the possibility of food and showers. We made our way to the World Food Program where, despite no food or sleep for two days, we tried to find a mechanic to go back through the Damra with us to claim our car before it was annexed by one or other of the militias. Standing around making calls on satellite phones, unshaven and unwashed after ten gruelling days in the field, we suddenly found ourselves in the middle of a delegation that included the newly appointed global head of the World Food Program. In fact, we were so well-placed that we formed a grotty and accidental greeting committee: shaking hands, smiling, welcoming the dignitaries to the compound in front of innumerable cameramen, coiffed PR officers and other equally pomaded lackeys dug up for the occasion. After three arduous weeks in the desert, a passing witness to the imbecility and human cost of war, I stood for a moment in front of one of the most influential humanitarians in the world.

'Where's my yoghurt?' she said …

CHAPTER 9
DISASTERS AND
CONFLICT

WHILE THE PAKISTAN earthquake had seemed to some extent solvable, armed conflict presents a deeper challenge to the ambitions of humanitarians. Natural disasters are classified as 'complicated' while conflicts are deemed 'complex'. In the earthquake, despite the many challenges, there was a sense that emergency needs, at least, were to some extent finite. A particular number of homes had been lost, a specific number of people had been affected. Therefore, if the relief effort went well and was well-funded, emergency needs could be met—the technocratic thinking that underpins the actions of every relief agency and funds a growing number of disaster statisticians, information managers, epidemiologists and demographers.

Conflict is different and altogether murkier. When I stood on top of that Muzaffarabad rubbish pile and was offered a job working in Darfur, I was told that this was a place where we were 'really needed'. But in conflict, the calculations of disaster statisticians matter less and are used indicatively—to paint a picture, rather than to guide the response. When I arrived in Darfur in 2007, estimates of the humanitarian consequences of the war varied. Initially, 200,000 had been killed in the fighting but this figure seemed too low. It was increased in 50,000 increments over the months to 250,000 before finally averaging out at 350,000. The point was not about the figures but to say that, no matter how accurate they were, they were morally incalculable. Each number represented a brutal, preventable enumeration of each individual death and loss. No known measure exists to quantify brutality, and statistics are brushstrokes in the portrayal of destruction. The vagueness of numbers (except for those of the agencies that keep detailed records of how many people they are feeding or providing medical treatment, which in any case only poorly symbolise an event) was an indication of the uncertainty of humanitarian agencies. The 'solutions' to the Darfur crisis did not lie in tents and tarpaulins, food distributions or medical programs, life-saving though these interventions are, but in the political and military calculations made by the Sudanese state and its militia allies—policies over which no aid agency has any influence.

In an African context, this portrayal—while true—had troubling repercussions. In the West, Africa was increasingly seen as an ongoing humanitarian crisis in itself, only newsworthy when there was 'another' major humanitarian catastrophe affecting hundreds of thousands of people. People noticeably talked about events 'in Africa' rather than naming the countries or contexts in which they occurred, overlooking regional differences, languages, cultures or other specificities. More frightening still was the language of barbarism that continued to underpin liberal concern about conflicts on the continent. 'Why are African conflicts so brutal?' asked a well-meaning friend, suggesting that there was a unique level of violence not experienced elsewhere—a kind of amnesia about the brutality of European history hidden behind the apparent order of wealthy societies.

This kind of thinking informed equally simplistic views about African conflicts: that they could be easily resolved through the intervention of 'capable' Western forces (Romeo Dallaire, commander of UN forces in Rwanda, propagated the myth that 5000 trained and equipped Western troops could have stopped the genocide); that conflicts are based on supposedly ancient ethnic and tribal tensions; and that development could be guided by the supposedly benign tutelage of Western aid agencies. 'Buy a goat,' runs the fundraising message associated with so many aid agencies, and you can 'solve world poverty'. There was more than a grain of truth in the observation of Jomo Kenyatta, the first president of independent Kenya, about 'those professional friends of the African who are prepared to maintain their friendship for eternity as a sacred duty, provided only that the African will continue to play the part of the ignorant savage so that they can monopolize the office of interpreting his mind and speaking for him'.

A problem for humanitarian agencies working in conflict arises because they are often seen—and encourage people to see them—as bearers of a moral or ethical flame. They carry the weight of moral expectation from their donors and the engaged citizens of wealthier countries who genuinely want to see an end to conflict or a focus on long-term investment to reduce poverty. Yet in conflicts these agencies have limited, if any, scope or authority to do more than provide basic humanitarian services that will not ultimately affect the political or economic causes of war.

Some agencies, like Oxfam or Médecins Sans Frontières (MSF), use public denunciation to influence policies that their operational activities cannot. Others, like the International Committee of the Red Cross (ICRC), with its hallowed tradition of Swiss neutrality, place priority on access to vulnerable people and so will only rarely comment publicly on the political motives that cause war and destruction. Along with private advocacy, the Red Cross pursues a narrower humanitarian agenda to try, against the odds, to ensure that civilians receive emergency life-saving assistance and are not targeted by any of the armed forces in a conflict. In a legal nicety, the ICRC therefore supports the Rome Statute (the basis in international law for the establishment of the International Criminal Court, which prosecutes genocide and crimes against humanity). The ICRC has a special exemption from appearing before the court itself or providing trial evidence based on the conduct of the conflicts in which it works. Unlike more advocacy-based assistance organisations, it supports the law but not the lawyers and judges who administer it or the invariable political consequences of the court's decisions.

It is in conflict situations that the humanitarian ideal runs into the most difficulty. Some have argued that humanitarianism is beginning to take the place of ideology in a post–Cold War world infatuated with international law and other technocratic solutions to complex political, ethical and historical problems. In the past, activists have sought to change society radically for the better: to gain independence; to afford rights, protection and representation; to ensure justice and equality before the crushing wheels of the market or the majority. Humanitarianism, in its proper form, does none of these things—it only attempts to make things less worse. It is an extension of, and an improvement upon, the condescending but still prevalent concept of charity. For many NGOs and in university courses, the term 'humanitarianism' is magically imbued with the rump of liberal causes and ideas. In this view, humanitarian action can somehow promote human rights, stop wars, and further social justice. Although it touches on all of these things, humanitarianism is a practice—often a technical and technocratic response to people with immediate life-preserving needs. It cannot change the political, social, and cultural landscape in which humanitarian action takes place, no matter how appalling the situation. It is the provision of band-aids magnified to the thousandth degree. In some cases this is sufficient. But in many, if not most, situations humanitarian action falls woefully short of the moral, political and financial commitments needed to preserve life, dignity and the environment in the longer term. Humanitarian work is a limited mechanism that is often overburdened with expectations of a solution that it simply cannot provide. Something that becomes even more problematic when, as in Afghanistan, almost all of the relief agencies (with the exceptions of MSF and the ICRC) were entirely funded by the governments of the belligerent powers.

On Pakistan Day, August 2007, I escaped from the confinement of our ring-fenced office where the pressures of work and the cautions of overzealous security officers had us imprisoned in 'lockdown'. Public holidays, religious festivals, meetings and gatherings of any sort—even Friday afternoon prayers—sent the ex-marine security officers from the UN Department of Safety and Security into paroxysms of fear. We were told to 'reduce our profile', take down flags and markings, park cars in the 'go' position, and for days and weeks on end we could not leave the secure compound with its high concrete walls and sleeping guards. Often alone in the office and annoyed by these restrictions, which I felt were completely unjustified, I made it my daily task to breach protocol in some way. At first this was a short lunchtime walk around the neighbourhood, which soon developed into chats with the local shop owners and an occasional game of street cricket. During lockdown, colleagues would sometimes come—strictly against orders—to keep me company and to continue to work in the best way we could, until finally Pakistan Day drew near and I was presented with an offer I could not refuse.

On this day, once a year, Pakistan Rail ran a celebratory train ride from the grand Saracen Gothic central station in Peshawar through the Khyber Pass and down to the border with Afghanistan. I had been invited to stop off along the way to have lunch at the mess of the famous Khyber Rifles regiment, where a colleague's brother was stationed. I was bored and this seemed the ideal way to break the lockdown monotony. So we hired a taxi and for a jittery moment I hid in the boot to avoid detection at the fairly cursory military road checks before starting on the road to Peshawar. It was sheer joy: the oppression of largely solitary confinement was behind me as we sped away from the village towards the tumult of Pakistan's most exciting city.

When I arrived at the station I was confronted with the sight of a beautiful nineteenth-century steam engine shunting and tooting into view. Uniformed attendants scurried around, enthusiastically waving flags and blowing whistles. Amid waving of streamers, cheering onlookers on the platform, and whistling and hooting from the train we wheezed out of the station, past serried rows of eucalypts and out onto the Gandhara plain towards Afghanistan. Knowing that I would lose my job immediately if anyone found out I had run away, I slid down in a seat at the back and was soon lost in a dreamlike state, gazing out onto the stretches dun-coloured plain and the pale blue of the Frontier sky.

'Come with me,' someone said enthusiastically, shaking me from my reverie. 'You can't sit here all the time, it's much more fun at the front.' I followed, head slightly bowed to preserve my anonymity, trying not to make eye contact with the Independence Day revellers. We walked through several carriages before coming out into the shaking, clanking engine room, where the driver was busy cranking up the temperature, closely monitoring it through an ancient brass gauge. With a nod and a shaking of hands, we climbed out of the train as it slowly gathered speed, clinging on to a railing at the side of the engine, and clawed our way through bursts of steam and dust up to a small ledge in front of the train. And there I sat for the next five hours, in front of a hurtling steam train watching the vast plains fold into the mountain passes that divide Pakistan from Afghanistan, thundering through villages and careening into seemingly unending tunnels as we made our way through the tribal no man's land of the Frontier. It was the ride of lifetime, enlivened by hordes of children who pounded the train with rocks as we passed. I discussed this with my new friend who had suggested this caper—did the pleasure of riding in front of the train outweigh the pain of being hit by a speeding rock?

'Yes,' was the immediate and unhesitating reply, 'although if they look like hitting us, you can dive under the grille and I'll turn my back.' With this plan of action and a sudden surge in speed, I felt reassured. 'Let's just hope they don't start shooting,' he added after a well-timed pause to set my nerves on edge again, and pointed out that many of the small rock-throwing boys were also carrying the ubiquitous Frontier Kalashnikov.

As Peshawar slowly vanished into the distance, a new political, social and economic reality became evident. We were now beyond the 'writ of the state'—in the tribal areas that form so much of the land of what was then know as the North West Frontier Province. These areas were self-governing, and the resources of the state, such as they were, had ceased to exist. There was no electricity and only one road, which ran alongside parts of the train track; there was no law enforcement, hence the almost compulsory bearing of arms by men and boys. Even the villages were different: settlements constructed from the dust mud and daub of the local environment were built around family compounds, each with high windowless perimeter fences and a tall watchtower. They were small family-based fortifications rather than houses in the more conventional sense. Instead of greeting the strangers who were now travelling bizarrely through their midst on a steam train, the locals met this intrusion initially with rocks, smashing as many windows as possible, before those inside the carriages could pull down the specially constructed wire screens, until at last the train came to a halt and smiling childish faces immediately leap off the embankments and formed a cheery welcome party for the strangers they had been attacking a moment before. In the distance I heard a high-pitched wheeze followed by a cacophony of shrieks and increasingly dominant drumming. And over the brow of a nearby hill, the massed bagpipes and drums of the Khyber Rifles Regiment appeared led by a stick-twirling drum-major dressed in a lion skin, from inside whose great jaws he shouted warlike musical commands.

'Are you Tom?' said a voice at my elbow amid the blare of bagpipes and the chatter of the frontier rock-throwers. 'I'm afraid Captain Shahab is fighting today but he has left instructions that you are to be our guest,' and I was presented with a curved dagger. And with that, covered in dust and soot and eyes still wild and bloodshot from the charging train, I was led clutching a gleaming steel knife to an ancient green jeep and driven to another army mess—an oasis of green, with manicured lawns bordered with roses and lazily resplendent peacocks. Inside, I toured the photo gallery, an unlikely who's who of the twentieth century with every president, prime minister, king and shah imaginable having visited the Khyber Rifles, whose HQ's strategic location had made it important on a world scale—a sort of South Asian Berlin Wall.

'Come,' said my new host. 'I'll show you the sights.'

He was not joking. We took the jeep to the top of a nearby hill and through the rangerfinder of a Pakistan Army howitzer I got my first breathtaking glimpse of the awesome mountain beauty of Afghanistan. Through the rangefinder I could see every detail of the border checks occurring at the Tulkarem border as people and cars passed through. For ease of artillery direction, each hill had been marked with a clearly visible number in white stone. It was a hair-raising moment as I stood, not on a geological fault line that had caused an earthquake, but on a geopolitical frontline that had so dramatically shaped the politics of the present.

Afghanistan is in many ways the Achilles heel of humanitarianism. It is a war that draws on, unwinnable—as so many invaders had found for centuries before 9/11—and it is a war that places aid agencies in the position of working alongside the armies of governments they are often so dependent on for funding. 'We're all on the same side, after all,' one military official in Islamabad said when questioned about the humanitarian consequences of the invasion. While I never crossed the border into Afghanistan, I was familiar with the ramifications of the war on our work in Pakistan. The Norwegian government, which funded my own aid agency, had made a decision to make troop deployments to Afghanistan and debate ensued among outraged colleagues as we came under pressure to work alongside

Norwegian troops as parts of an NGO 'hearts and minds' campaign. Here civilians were seen, in crude Pentagon terminology, as 'force multipliers': organisations that would extend the reach, influence, and legitimacy of the 'liberators' and who, in the words of another commander, would 'win it for us'.

But if the NGOs were concerned about cooptation to broader military goals, armies themselves wasted no time learning development-speak and employing the controversial Provincial Reconstruction Teams (PRTs) with enormous funds to engage in pseudo-development projects designed partly to rebuild civilian infrastructure and partly to create goodwill—sometimes in exchange for political information and intelligence sharing. But in obvious conjunction with military ends, these development programs were inherently tainted and frequently mistrusted. Based largely on the need to spend cash and buy favour rather than on sound development principles, their funds and effort went on white elephant projects that blurred the lines between independent humanitarian assistance and military strategy: school buildings without teachers, for example. In one province five MSF aid workers were killed by the Taliban because they were accused, falsely, by the local commander of 'spying for America'. On pulling out of Afghanistan following the attacks, MSF stated that 'independent humanitarian action, which involves unarmed aid workers going into areas of conflict to provide aid, has become impossible.'

The development of new military 'doctrines'—'hearts and minds', 'force multipliers', and the 3D approach (in which armies were involved across the spectrum of work from defence and diplomacy to development)—added to deepening and at times fatal unease about the future of neutral and impartial humanitarian space. The political pressure and financial incentives to be on the 'same side' were intense.

Despite the generosity of my hosts and the sparkling late afternoon on the regimental lawns, I suddenly felt tired. I had escaped the tedium of lockdown more than I ever imagined, but having moved briefly among the military side of the humanitarian divide I felt a deep urge to get back on the train and head as fast as I could to my own compound and to aid work delivered on the basis of need rather than political or military objectives.

CHAPTER 10
MISSIONARIES, MERCENARIES AND MISFITS

JOSIAH WEDGEWOOD'S 1787 medallion advocating the abolition of the slave trade is emblazoned with the famous line: 'Am I not a man and a brother?' It features an African man in chains, down on one knee, raising his hands together in supplication. This urgent appeal to humanitarian universality, 'man and brother', is made by the benighted poor, who in Wedgewood's view could be liberated from the economic chains of slavery and set free by religious conversion. It illustrates a significant departure from the amoral commercial mentality that dominated the Western empires until the end of the eighteenth century and lingered well into the nineteenth.

The campaign for the abolition of the slave trade was one of the great humanitarian achievements of the nineteenth century, yet it also granted ethical legitimacy to Western imperial expansion. Echoing themes in aid and development practice today, early humane societies sought to liberate Africans from oppression while staking the claim of imperial powers to govern the continent as they liberated souls.

In a contradiction that has dogged humanitarian work from the outset, the poor and those affected by conflict and disasters are often seen by aid agencies and charitable institutions as being both in need of a saviour and, to some degree, there for the taking. Disasters, in this view, can be seen as opportunities: to change behaviour, to reimagine a long-term future amid the destruction of the old, and to gain access and influence. For secular institutions, there is often an interventionist rhetoric of 'change, development and empowerment'; for religious ones there is the desire, ultimately, to convert the people they help by promoting something called 'human transformation'—in the language of World Vision, by 'bearing witness to the good news of the Kingdom of God'.

Both these views, as well as the starker humanitarian commitment of the Red Cross to uphold the laws of war, owe their origins to the universalised conceptions of aid and charity that arose during the nineteenth century. While assistance and charity were by no means new—neighbourhood associations, trade and manufacturing guilds, and associations of almsgivers had existed in varying forms for hundreds of years—the great revolutions of the eighteenth century had begun to suggest the language, if not the content, of a universal political and ethical ambition. The American Declaration of Independence invoked the idea of 'inalienable rights' to life, liberty and the pursuit of happiness, which it found 'self-evident'; this was echoed in the French Declaration of the Rights of Man and the Citizen, in which rights were deemed 'natural, unalienable and sacred' and, more specifically, amounted to 'liberty, property, security and resistance to oppression'. While these declarations radically paved the way for more rational and secular state structures, they were also exactly what they appeared—rights for 'man and the citizen', in which there was no apparent contradiction between espousing the pursuit of happiness and owing slaves or having an inalienable right to freedom from oppression while maintaining slave-run sugar plantation colonies such as Haiti; meanwhile, rights for women could wait another 150 years.

The modern humanitarian ideal is consequently a curious mid-nineteenth-century amalgam of state-sponsored imperial expansion, the professionalisation of military medicine, the rise of evangelical religion and the universalising ideals of the great eighteenth-century revolutions (Jean-Jacques Rousseau could write in the middle of the eighteenth century about an 'innate repugnance at seeing a fellow creature suffer'). The rise of colonialism in the nineteenth century was also linked to the 'passion for compassion' that underpins contemporary humanitarian action.

Contemporary ideas about international assistance have emerged from humanitarianism's complex historical traditions, and despite claims to the universality of human needs and suffering, humanitarian organisations reflect their ideologically and institutionally eclectic past. In the post–Cold War world, in which aid agencies have increasingly taken on the role of guardians of public conscience, these origins are problematic—they pose challenges where ideological position, political positioning and dependence on donor funding undercut claims to universal and impartial humanitarian assistance delivered on the basis of need rather than other ideological, religious or political imperatives.

Just as there is an increasing professionalisation of aid delivery, in a bizarre move agencies and governments have started to redefine core concepts of humanitarian assistance along Orwellian lines. Meeting with officials from AusAID, the Australian aid agency, I was informed that the agency's humanitarian policy was based around the principles of 'humanity, independence, neutrality, and impartiality'—core humanitarian concepts derived from the Fundamental Principles of the Red Cross and Red Crescent Movement. Yet it is also a government agency formally operating in the 'national interest' in conjunction with Australia's foreign policy objectives—a fact that has been underlined, in a breathtakingly retrograde step, with the agency's recent abolition and absorption into the Australian Department of Foreign Affairs. 'Disaster relief', as Henry Kissinger noted in an American context as early as 1976, 'is becoming increasingly a major instrument of our foreign policy'.

Unstated in the desire to do good works that bring respect and legitimacy to the doer is the equally important need to be seen to be acting. The predominance of logos, hoardings and awnings advertise the generosity of the aid agencies and their donors with ever greater assertiveness in refugee camps and settlements for the internally displaced after disasters. It has become increasingly important, if you are a beneficiary of aid and need access to emergency food, shelter or other basic necessities, to know that this aid ultimately comes from the British/Australian/American people. The moral sanctity of aid confers goodwill, legitimacy, and ultimately and most importantly a 'seat at the table'—and thus influence for the delivering agencies and governments that fund them.

This moral and political power is part of the daily terrain that aid agencies must navigate in order to remain genuinely neutral, and it is complicated by frequent financial dependence on partisan donors—such as governments, the military or private philanthropic organisations. Such dependence has seen aid agencies adopt numerous counterpositions in order to guarantee their independence. These have included raising revenue independently through regular donations, of which the most spectacularly successful has been 'child sponsorship', as well as making conscience-based appeals for public funding in order to respond to emergencies. Both these activities, however, are fraught—the expropriation of the images of children and the portrayal of suffering to shock audiences into making donations is understandable but problematic. 'Only compassion sells,' as an aid worker from the French aid agency Action Against Hunger said. 'It is the basis of fundraising for humanitarian agencies. We can't seem to do without it.'

In their search for identity and points of distinction that might impress donors, core support groups or the public,

NGOs have devised a series of stances and positions: some idealistic and ambitious, some technocratic, and some faith-based appeals to higher powers, all of which range from the admirable to the cant—'mission statements', in the fused missionary, military and business terminology of the aid world. Oxfam, for example, takes a rights-based approach that seeks to empower individuals and communities and to provide the material means for people to make meaningful choices about who they are and how they live. Oxfam's 'mission statement' says that:

> *Oxfam's vision is a just world without poverty. We envision a world in which people can influence decisions which affect their lives, enjoy their rights, and assume their responsibilities as full citizens of a world in which all human beings are valued and treated equally.*

In contrast, World Vision announces its intentions in a form of religious incantation whose humanitarian agenda is openly evangelical. Rather than attempting to create a world in which the people living in poverty have power over their future, World Vision draws deeply on Christian traditions of the benighted poor. Despite the sophistication of some of this well-funded organisation's aid programs, its goals are other-worldly ones that are aimed to promote (preferably Christian) spiritual wellbeing rather than, for example, mere access to safe drinking water:

> *Our vision for every child, life in all its fullness;*

> *Our prayer for every heart, the will to make it so.*

World Vision is an international partnership of Christians whose mission is to follow our Lord and Savior Jesus Christ in working with the poor and oppressed to promote human transformation, seek justice, and bear witness to the good news of the Kingdom of God.

At odds with both Oxfam's empowerment approach and World Vision's evangelising mission through good works, the International Committee of the Red Cross (ICRC) sees itself as the grandfather clock of humanitarianism, whose stately but resonant ticking echoes through the generations to remind humanitarians of the essential imperatives of their cause. The oldest and largest humanitarian organisation, the ICRC and the Red Cross Movement more generally is the institution mandated under the Geneva Conventions to uphold the 'laws of war', which support the key elements of neutrality and impartiality of humanitarian actors in armed conflict. In keeping with this legal mandate the ICRC describes itself in the following way:

an impartial, neutral and independent organization whose exclusively humanitarian mission is to protect the lives and dignity of victims of armed conflict and other situations of violence and to provide them with assistance. The ICRC also endeavours to prevent suffering by promoting and strengthening humanitarian law and universal humanitarian principles.

With its origins as an offshoot of ICRC, Médecins Sans Frontièrs (MSF) sought to bring to humanitarian action the ICRC's technical expertise in emergency medicine combined with a critique of the neutrality provision that, at the height of 1960s activism, had seemed an archaic hangover from the nineteenth century. What would distinguish MSF from being co-opted by the establishment or remaining silent when there was an overwhelming moral imperative to speak out was the principle of *témoignage,* 'bearing witness'. Coming as something of a relief following various attempts at ever greater worthiness, the neo-classical arch of the MSF office in the Netherlands supports a mock portentious Latin phrase. Carved into the architrave, it is at once a call to action and a witty critique of an older version of humanitarian action: *Homo sapiens non urinat in ventrum* (People should not piss into the wind). Like the ICRC, and unlike organisations such as Oxfam and World Vision, MSF takes a minimalist definition of humanitarian action. In the words of MSF's Christophe Fournier:

> *Our ambition is a limited one. Our purpose is not to bring war to an end. Nor is it humanitarian to build state and government legitimacy or to strengthen governmental structures. It's not to promote democracy or capitalism or women's rights. Not to defend human rights or save the environment. Nor does humanitarian action involve the work of economic development, post-conflict reconstruction. Or the establishment of functioning health systems. It is about saving lives and alleviating suffering in the immediate term. What we do in Afghanistan is for today. We heal people for the sake of healing people.*

But sometimes, the pressing practical and ethical concerns and the ideological ambitions of aid agencies can become a burden on humanitarian workers, especially when returning from 'the field'. How does one attempt to explain the intricacies of humanitarian action in far-off places? Returning to headquarters on R&R from the field, I found myself responding to well-meant questions like 'How are things over there?', and worse still, 'What do you do?' with increasingly elaborate ways of avoiding the question. Some humanitarian workers on trips home said they were architects, teachers or engineers and used their professional backgrounds as camouflage, while others invented detailed alternative lives as insurance brokers, hairdressers, bar tenders, or, *in extremis*, claims to golfing celebrity. Above all, our return home brings the strange realisation of the moral sentiment attached to humanitarian work, after being engaged in the often brutal, matter-of-fact reality of work on the ground. Someone rattling the tin for NGO donations on the street once accosted me as I was waiting for a bus. 'Would you like to be a humanitarian superhero?' Fresh from Sudan, having witnessed everything but the romantic view of overseas aid work, I made my excuses and ran as far as I could. At the time, the word 'Darfur' seemed to have an electric impact on those who heard it—it was the cause of the moment, 'our Spain', as one friend had put it before I left—but this was far from the complex reality of that brutal desert war that raised so many questions that were beyond the ability, scope and resources of humanitarian organisations to meet. The gritty realities of humanitarian action on the ground were a world away from the cartoon version of 'superheros' being peddled on the streets to raise revenue. It was an uncomfortable disjuncture between the ideals of aid agencies and reality of aid workers that often seemed incommunicable to those who had not been there. Finding out that someone had been to one or two of the grimmer 'missions' tended to evoke, if anything, a sense of relief among others who had experienced the same thing—a sort of returned aid worker phenomenon—which sometimes formed a tacit understanding. In the strangely pseudo-military language of relief agencies: a stint in the field meant you had, as I was told, 'earnt your stripes'.

CHAPTER 11
FORCE MULTIPLIERS AND HUMANITARIAN MILITANTS

IN A RECENT TV INTERVIEW, an Australian Army commander in Afghanistan talked about building schools, women's rights and empowering communities in language that, if I closed my eyes and didn't see the dun-coloured khaki uniform, could just as easily have emerged from the mouth of seasoned aid worker. While I was working in Pakistan there was much hand-wringing discussion (especially for colleagues based over the border in Afghanistan) about whether one European institution I worked for would direct its humanitarian activities to areas in which its government had supplied troops—what we saw as humanitarian assistance, embassy and military officials referred to as 'force multipliers'.

This was a term used by the unfortunately named US Defense Department official David Kilcullen, a guerilla warfare specialist. Kincullen's book *Accidental Guerrilla: Fighting Small Wars in the Middle of a Big One* advanced the idea that what was needed was a an 'ethnography of conflict', in which the invading belligerents themselves as well as coopted NGOs play the role of 'participant observer' who could understand 'the way they act and think'. In this deeply dangerous and misguided conception, medical NGOs are key to the process of incorporating development principles of participation and ethnography into ways of winning counterinsurgency wars. Humanitarian actors are seen as 'force multipliers', or the 'Build' component of the military catechism for winning counterinsurgency wars: *Shape, Clear, Hold, Build.*

Militaries were increasingly coopting the work of humanitarian agencies, especially in places like Afghanistan, but this was not an entirely new phenomenon. In contrast to their British and French counterparts, which tended to emerge from left-leaning civil society opposition to the state, American relief agencies shared close funding and ideological relationships with the government. CARE (Cooperative for American Remittances to Europe, whose origins lay in the relief and reconstruction effort after World War II) and Catholic Relief Services (CRS) were two of the largest and best-funded aid organisations during the Cold War. Having been major recipients of US government funding following World War II, both CARE and CRS developed close relationships with government, which were consolidated with both the lure of additional funding and ideological opposition to communism during the Cold War. During the

Vietnam war, this led CRS in particular to ally itself with the anti-communist Catholics who made up a significant component of the South Vietnamese government in Saigon that was being funded and militarily propped up by the US. CIA-funded humanitarian operations were justified on the basis that, according to CRS itself, 'this relief was actually an integral part of a well-conceived strategy of building support for the reactionary Saigon government in order to avert the widely predicted victory of Ho Chi Minh'. CARE received similar funding and shared CRS and CIA's objectives, although was not also motivated by religious factors. Both institutions 'endorsed the government's foreign aid strategy and worked to contain communism and promote American ideas and institutions' during the Cold War. In the post–Cold War period, both CRS and CARE lost their partisan funding and ideological dependency on the US government, and now more closely resemble rights-based NGOs. CRS began to realign itself with progressive Catholic social teaching rather than the faith's more conservative traditions. However, debates about the cooptation of NGOs for military and foreign policy purposes, were being carried out a full forty years before this occurred in Afghanistan.

While some institutions worked closely with government, others—especially those based in Britain and France—derived from a progressive and sometimes socialist tradition. Institutions such as Oxfam, Save the Children and MSF, for example, saw themselves as being oppositional to the aims of the state and a moral voice calling governments to account over policies and practices that were self-interested rather than humane. Save the Children started, controversially, by advocating for relief efforts to relieve civilian suffering in former enemy states (Germany and the ex–Austro-Hungarian Empire) with whom Britain had been at war during World War I, while the Biafran conflict in Nigeria in the late 1960s galvanised Oxfam's international position and led to the birth of MSF.

In the context of 1960s social revolution, the rise of television and mass media, and the decolonisation of Africa, the Biafran conflict struck a particularly acute chord. Seeking its own independence from the recently independent unitary Nigerian state, the ethnic Igbo-Hausa–dominated area of Biafra claimed separate statehood. What followed was a bloody postcolonial war that included brutal military offensives and blockades which, combined with disruptions to markets and agriculture, led to the death of more than two million Biafrans. British government policy was to provide tacit support to the Nigerian government. British policy viewed the Nigerian government as both the 'legitimate' successor to the colonial administration and, in order to preserve multiethnic Nigerian unity as a counterbalance to French-dominated West Africa, to assert post-imperial influence. In this official view, the Biafran conflict represented a civil war or secession rather than an ethnically based conflict targeting civilians that was tantamount to genocide.

As famine threatened a further eight million Biafrans and images of starvation reached Western audiences, traditional humanitarian values of neutrality began to appear insufficient to address the urgent humanitarian and moral imperatives of preventing mass death. In the absence of British government support, Oxfam proved particularly effective in public advocacy and organised mass campaigns in opposition to the British government's position and in order to raise funds directly to mount a relief operation. Just as it did in supporting Live Aid concerts to raise money for famine relief in Ethiopia in the 1980s, organisations such as Oxfam embodied the progressive view of aid agencies and institutions that uncovered the truth for an engaged public and used this support to speak it to power. In doing so, Oxfam embodied the moral authority—often in opposition to the established authorities—that has been attributed to aid agencies ever since.

Similarly, the founders of MSF, among them Bernard Kouchner, began their humanitarian careers as volunteer doctors with ICRC, the institution responsible for the very concepts of impartiality, neutrality and independence. But by the 1960s with growing, if somewhat belated, recognition of the Holocaust, ICRC's preservation of nineteenth-century humanitarian codes seemed to indicate irresponsibility if not actual complicity in mass atrocity. ICRC, despite having access to Nazi concentration camps, and having won the Nobel Peace Prize for its humanitarian work with prisoners of war, had not spoken out against the greatest crime of the age. As Simone Deorenzi has written, 'the ICRC continued for the most part to operate as an amateur with relatively modest objectives; when attacked for its passive stance vis-à-vis the concentration camps, its standard response was to side-step the issue, refusing to examine the implications of its silence'.

For Kouchner, whose own grandparents had died in Auschwitz, the parallels between ICRC silence during World War II and the vast scale of the Biafran conflict in which ICRC also retained its code of silence were too obvious to be tolerated. He and fellow ICRC-volunteer doctor Max Recamier founded MSF—an organisation that would provide medical support in the same way as ICRC and retaining much of the minimalist humanitarian ethic of the organisation.

This was a new concept, it was hoped, that would allow MSF to continue working in much the same way as ICRC but would also allow it to move beyond the restrictions of the ICRC's approach and engage in the moral-humanitarian questions of the day. In practice, however, MSF found itself in a similar dilemma to the Red Cross—as medical professionals, its doctors were bound by confidentiality, and relative political silence on moral issues meant guaranteed access to vulnerable people that would have been denied by the Nigerian government had the organisation criticised it too strongly. Almost immediately, Kouchner fell foul with the emerging MSF consensus and went on to found another French medical NGO, Médecins du Monde, which was closer to his more engaged conception of humanitarian assistance. As Kouchner himself wrote: 'I am a political militant. How can one be a humanitarian militant if one is not political? It is the same thing for me'.

For me, the limitations of humanitarian work seemed evident in Darfur. Despite the urgency of the needs, the humanitarian problems there were not those that humanitarian work alone could solve. It was a political, historical and humanitarian mess, and when I returned to Australia I advocated, briefly, for the greatest humanitarian contradiction in terms—'humanitarian intervention' with the use of military force to put a stop to … a humanitarian crisis. It was a view that was as tempting as it was simplistic, and one that revealed the limitations of both the worldly aspirations that progressive humanitarian ideals would triumph but which failed to take into account complex, newly emerging political and historical realities in places such as Sudan, Pakistan and Afghanistan.

The word 'humanitarian' can and is often used to indicate its exact opposite. While it has been used to justify going to war on humanitarian grounds, what is clear is that 'humanitarianism' has now developed into a fundamental political, social and cultural concept. In Australia, the ultimate irony of respective governments' preoccupation with asylum seekers arriving by boat is that the inhuman and illegal measures used to deter them from coming to the Lucky Country, including incarceration for indeterminate periods of time, are justified on humanitarian grounds because this will, allegedly, prevent asylum seekers from being exploited by ruthless boat owners seeking to profit from their desperation to reach new countries. The well-established human and humanitarian rights to seek asylum when fleeing from well-founded fears of persecution are, in local political terms, trumped by the 'humanitarian' good of stopping asylum seekers from undertaking dangerous voyages in the first place. Here, an ostensibly humanitarian principle is used to justify its opposite. Humanitarianism, in all its different and sometimes contradictory forms and guises, is in many ways the problematic ethical and political logic adopted by governments and aid agencies when confronted with a breakdown of order—in disasters and wars; when dealing with the socially marginalised or refugees. For aid agencies and governments humanitarian work is a convoluted mix of altruism, notions of compassion and ethical responsibility, human-rights promotion and political self-interest. Humanitarianism is, in many ways, the nebulous logic of our age.

One of the most remarkable things about the idea of humanitarianism is that it has such a multiplicity of uses and meanings. It can be used to justify both progressive and reactionary causes, can be pro- or anti-government, and can aspire to being the moral voice of a generation while also manipulating the images and needs of vulnerable people in order to maximise revenue, albeit for the good of the cause. Ultimately, humanitarianism can also include its opposite—military intervention on humanitarian grounds. As David Rieff has written in *A Bed for the Night* [4]:

> *what we discern in it (humanitarianism) we have come looking for, and its plasticity as a concept consoles us. There is the humanitarian as noble caregiver, as dupe to power, as designated conscience, as revolutionary, as colonialist, as business man, and perhaps even as mirror. There is humanitarianism as caring, as in Rwanda; humanitarianism as emancipation, as in Afghanistan after the fall of the Taliban; humanitarianism as liberation, as in the case for humanitarian support for the rebels of southern Sudan; and humanitarianism as counterinsurgency, as it as in Vietnam and may yet be again in Afghanistan.*

---

[4] David Rieff, *A Bed for the Night*, Vintage, New York, 2002, p. 88

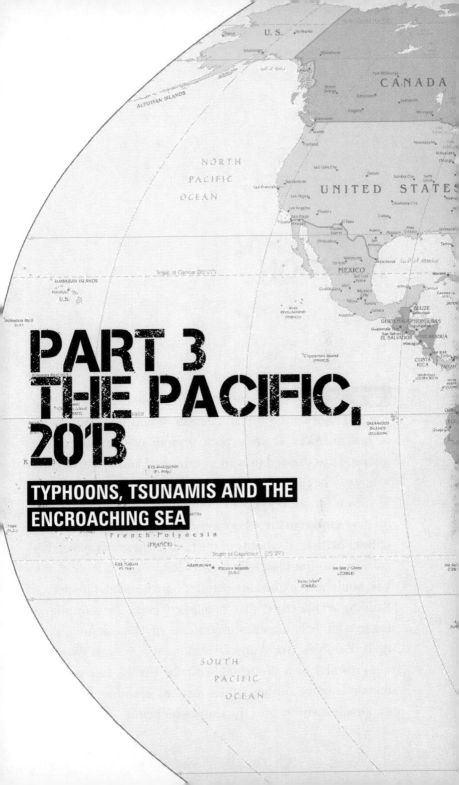

PART 3
THE PACIFIC,
2013

TYPHOONS, TSUNAMIS AND THE
ENCROACHING SEA

CHAPTER 12
TYPHOON

I TOOK THE CALL from the antique dilapidation of the San Tango Hotel in the bohemian San Telmo neighbourhood of Buenos Aires. It was a bizarre moment—at that precise instant, I was dressed only in a bath towel and was struggling to adjust a head torch while navigating a staircase in the dark. The San Tango 'bohemian boutique', as it had advertised itself, was based in the self-professed artistic and musical heart of Buenos Aires, the home of the tango. There was a decaying grandeur to the place—both San Telmo and Buenos Aires. Vast boulevards named after triumphant generals intersected Parisian architecture that outclassed even the sumptuous haute-bourgeois imperial aspirations of Haussmann's Paris itself. This New World arrivisme along the Avenida Belgrano was crowned by a disturbingly phallic obelisk celebrating a military victory, no less, which cast an ominous shadow of nationalistic virility over the traffic jam below.

San Telmo was the opposite extreme to the pride, power and hubristic architecture of the centre. Narrow streets slowly revealed small squares filled with cafes and restaurants, each with its own professional tango couple—dancing for hours in a mesmerising swirl of 1940s glamour: heels, brilliantine, satin and pinstripe, enmeshed in a dance that fused the nocturnal passion of a sultry evening with the kinetic control and precision of the professional athlete. And for all the tango's famed eroticism, there was something professionally clinical about the street dancers. The tango itself was born in the brothels of nineteenth-century Buenos Aires and became popularised through its distinctive music and the haunting songs of its leading exponent, Carlos Gardel, whose Brylcreem-ed hair and dark 1940s suits remain the businessman–brothel-goer image of the tango dancer today. Despite its passion and great wallowing in the mourning and heartbreak of love and loss contained in its songs, the tango retains an element of detachment, an erotic reverie lined with remorse and the cold glint of cash. In 'Mi Buenos Aires querido' (My beloved Buenos Aires), Gardel sings of both the city and the girl with the melancholia typical of the tango:

The tiny windows of my streets of Arrabal,
Where a young girl gives a smile;
I want to stare once again
At those eyes that fondle with a look.
In the toughest back alley, a song
Says its prayer of courage and of passion;A promise
And a sigh
Wiped away a tear of sadness, that singing.

But what passed for bohemian in Buenos Aires was essentially the profound malaise of economic collapse in a place that was—within recent memory—strikingly successful. In the 'tough back alleys', dancers strutted for endless hours in front of occasional tourists, and from somewhere within the grot and decay was the ever present dank sweetness of the evening's weed. The San Tango Hotel was itself once a sturdy bourgeois home with elegant balconies and high ceilings. But gradually these pleasures wore thin—first the external window blind collapsed, leaving the room in pitch blackness. Then the electricity and the water went out simultaneously. I stumbled around trying to find my head torch in order to get dressed, and managed to feel my way downstairs in search of the owner. But she had left, locking the front door behind her, and I realised that I was trapped. There was no other way out and after I'd spent several hours sitting, waiting in the darkness, my phone rang.

'Greetings from Geneva,' said a friendly voice at the other end. 'There's been a typhoon in the Philippines—do you want to go to Mindanao?'

The magic word had been said. Of course I wanted to go to Mindanao—in my mind a complex and dangerous place and one interlinked with my earliest exhilarating exposure to Islamic civilisation. For many years while I was growing up in the Phillipines, my family home had been filled with furniture, lamps, tables and chairs whose unmistakable arabesque decoration hailed from Mindanao. Pictures on the walls showed Spanish Philippine life in the 1890s, especially 'postprandial scenes in Manila'—exhausted Peninsulares smoking great cigars and being waited on by attentive liveried servants in the heavy tropical heat of the night. The sofa had an elevated section under which visitors could keep their fighting cocks cordially separated while being entertained with tea and polite conversation. A colourful woven Philippine cloth was used for picnics, and our unsuspecting guests suffered in uncomfortable silence when they were told mid-canapé that it was, in fact, a shroud. As a child, I had even turned up at a birthday party in aviator glasses and a leather jacket posing as a bonsai General Douglas MacArthur—a midget American Caesar and Liberator of the Philippines (as MacArthur styled himself) appearing before a group of unsuspecting infants.

Mindanao was, in the late 1970s, off-limits—home to a deadly conflict between communist insurgents, Muslim separatists who had never quite succumbed to Spanish or American rule, and the stupendous smarminess and corruption of the Marcos regime. It was a brutal anti-communist US satellite state that, in a postcolonial twist, ensured its support from the former colonial master by substantially funding US Republicans—the despotic trunk wagging the elephant of the Grand Old Party.

It was a relationship of mutual reliance and admiration tinged with an almost postcolonial regret. Massive US bases in Subic Bay outside Manila were deemed strategically vital during the Cold War while successive Philippine regimes, not least that of Marcos, relied on American support and funding for legitimacy. But there was a legacy of direct American rule too, on which US claims to be a liberal progressive force for newly independent countries largely rested—a claim that the Philippines had been created, to quote the journalist Stanley Kurnow, 'in our own image', and that the country was the product of benign US tutelage. This mutually reinforcing self-regard filled the Reagan–Marcos relationship; as one State Department official later mused, the American president regarded Marcos like 'a hero from a bubble gum card he had collected as a kid'.

When my parents expressed their disapproval of the crew-cut conservatism of the regime and its US backers to an English colleague, she replied that they should simply ignore the 'depredations of the Hottentot'. Hers was the aloof response of the older empire to the apparent crassness of the new. Ironically, her early career in colonial Africa had been cut short when her husband was eaten by a crocodile while serving as a British district commissioner.

In the toxic dictatorial days of anti-communism and Marcos, my parents' liberalism was seen as an almost incendiary provocation. Accused of being pinkos and commies, over an unwise attempt to introduce Dostoevsky into the curriculum of the international school at which they taught, they became embroiled in a series of confrontations with rabidly anti-Russian, anti-communist authorities. This eventually culminated in a potentially dangerous altercation with the Philippines Long Distance Telephone Company over non-payment of an astronomical and largely fictitious bill. As the dispute escalated, threats were made to have the family's passports confiscated and visas revoked, and suggestions of implication in some communist plot were fabricated. An influential member of the Manila elite came to the rescue. In exchange for safe passage out of the country, my father would preside over the Philippines Long Distance Telephone Company Junior Executive Public Speaking Competition. This was a fate compounded by the fact that all the junior executives on the make were required to memorise and perform the same speech—José Rizal's speech supporting the independence of the Philippines, which begins with the faux-rhetorical question: 'What is a man?'

My unexpected return to the Philippines thirty years later found an altogether different country and circumstance. Typhoon Bopha, known locally as Typhoon Pablo, had smashed through the island of Mindanao in the southern Philippines, causing massive devastation. More than six million people had been affected, nearly one million left without homes, as the typhoon made landfall in Mindanao with wind speeds of up to 260 kilometres per hour. Driving through the wreckage when I arrived on the island, I saw palm trees that had been splintered like giant toothpicks, forests scattered across farms, fields and waterways, leaving roads blocked, gardens torn to shreds and houses smashed. In one area, Andaap, severe flooding caused giant boulders to wash downstream, diverting the local river—sweeping away entire villages in its path. Two thousand people died in the fast-moving river of rock. As the waters receded, they left a moonscape scar ripped through the farms and forests of Mindanao.

I arrived on the second rotation, replacing a colleague who had been there when the typhoon hit, as an emergency coordinator. The response had been going for a month but, as my predecessor said as we parted at the airport: 'Good luck—it's like swimming in treacle.' And he was exactly right—the humanitarian response that we were attempting to coordinate had all but stalled. Despite the endless hours I spent in meetings, listening to overawed government representatives and pushing donors, interest in the Philippines had largely tailed off. Nobody was interested in funding the response; international NGOs sat ready and waiting to gear up but had to make do with the pathetic resources that were slowly trickling in.

Major international organisations and their leading responders had circled for a brief moment after the typhoon, but the old hands had seen the writing on the wall early on and returned quickly to their strategic locales in Bangkok, Kuala Lumpur and New York. I found a note in a pile of old documents calling for the exalted names of international disaster response, O'Boosie and Panico. Representing major UN and NGO institutions, they were considered the only men capable of handling such a large-scale operation. But by the time I arrived, the heady days of the O'Boosie–Panico disaster response dream team in the Philippines were a distant memory and the long slog of another underfunded and half-forgotten response was left to lesser mortals.

'I know you've lost your house, but have a laminated sack,' mocked one of my colleagues in frustration at the deeply substandard relief supplies his agency was forced to distribute. The typhoon had occurred at exactly the wrong time—in early December, just as government, media, civil society and international donors were beginning to wind things up for the year. A CNN reporter arrived in Mindanao for just two days before being dispatched back to Bangkok, while several NGOs pooled funds to fly in the BBC, which didn't even have the budget to cover the event itself. Christmas in the irredeemably Catholic Philippines combined with the seasonal media black hole effectively blocked out any immediate coverage of the typhoon, after which it had become old news. Donors, already disengaged, had even less incentive to respond, even as heavy post-typhoon rains continued to cause widespread flooding—leading to the further displacement of 40,000 already homeless people. They camped by roadsides, saving basic possessions and tethering their prized fighting cocks to the barriers that lined the roads and highways, or took refuge in 'bunkhouses'—shabby plywood constructions unconnected to water, sanitation or drainage, which housed ten people to a room.

Trying to raise funds, I returned to Manila to meet with donors and to try to impress upon them the clear and immediate needs that still existed. From the wrecked coconut plantations and apocalyptic rockscape of Andaap, I was plunged into the heart of the Manila business district—a mini Singapore surrounded by high security, clusters of grey skyscrapers separated by unending, immobile lines of traffic. Through the barbed wire and concrete walls lining the freeway on the way in from the airport, glamorous half-European models looked out at the passing traffic advertising Pizza Hut or the latest kitchen range from enormous billboards bolted onto the roofs of the city's vast slums. At one particularly intractable intersection dominated by a tangle of telephone wires and yet more concrete flyovers, a grim billboard dominated the surroundings.

WE STRONGLY SUPPORT LETHAL INJECTION

It was advertising an insecticide. Further on, celebrating the overthrow of the Marcos regime by Corazon Aquino's People Power Movement, another banner read:

THE FILIPINO IS WORTH DYING FOR

The legend was written in the hand of Aquino's assassinated father, who had returned to the Philippines from exile in the US to campaign against the authoritarian corruption and cronyism of the Marcos regime. All over the city, neon signs on the tops of buildings flashed with the self-promoting religiosity of the American bank note: *In God We Trust*. Along the Manila's once stunning palm-fringed bay stood Asia's largest shopping mall. The enormous icerink at its centre cooled the boutiques for miles around as the middle classes learned the delicate arts of figure skating and ice-ballet. Located near some of Manila's extensive slums, this was—in the disturbingly euphemistic words of Imelda Marcos, who still wields influence from her seat in the Philippine senate—'a challenging transition from a traditional order to a progressive humanist society.'

While 'the Filipino' may have been worth dying for, they were certainly not, according to the donors I met, worth funding. Racing between offices in the small thicket of plate-glass towers housing embassies and United Nations offices in the heart of Manila's financial district, I found virtually identical unphased and unresponsive reactions to my pleas for assistance. Hermetically sealed behind bomb-proof doors, metal detectors and armed guards, diplomats and donors looked down on the humid, smog-filled city below. They were even further removed from it by the intense cold and thin air of viciously air-conditioned offices—a blood-less arctic stillness in the middle of South-East Asia.

'Shouldn't we see Typhoon Bopha as an opportunity?' I was asked in one office. The destruction of farms, houses and livelihoods along the Mindanao coast had swept away the potentially annoying 'human element' in future plans for beach resorts and mass tourism. Another international donor went into paroxysms of pleasure when I showed a handout which, quite by accident, had a picture with their logo on it. We should be promoting the private sector, someone else told me, instead of seeking aid 'handouts', while a man from Iowa instructed me about how he spent his holidays out on his farm with a chainsaw in hand and there was 'nothing to it'. What this meant I never really learned—after a long discussion about the virtues of self-reliance, I was told the US didn't fund United Nations humanitarian funding appeals anyway. Bush-era prejudices clearly survived in the lower reaches of the American administration. Crestfallen, I declined the offer of a frozen burrito and made my way out.

The opportunities and self-reliance advocated by donors in the capital meant something entirely different and more sinister in Mindanao itself. Before leaving for Manila, I had learned that 'recruiters' had sensed fertile ground and become active in the some of the affected areas—offering women, whose livelihoods had been destroyed in the disaster, contracts to work as domestic labour overseas. At $400 a month, these contracts were considered lucrative by many local people, despite the serious risk of physical, sexual and economic abuse they carry with them, not to mention the increased vulnerability of children and families left behind.

In areas where people had received help—notably, along the sides of main roads—there was evidence of rebuilding and early signs of recovery. Elsewhere, despite the mantra of the development community to 'build back better', people lived in makeshift shelters made from the debris of their former homes. The unaided majority who lived in the mud on the site of their original homes were building back worse. For one woman I met, whose home was a flooded tent, Typhoon Bopha had brought devastation. She had been given a tent by an aid agency but this had been inadvertently placed in an unshaded area prone to flooding. By herself with four small children, she had been unable to relocate the tent, which was too hot to use during the day. Instead, she was living with her children in the remains of her old house—a wooden shanty at the outer perimeter of the village, which at least provided some shade. She did have some assistance from a cousin, who had come to help look after the children. Some vulnerable groups, such as the elderly, were barely in a position to build back or to help themselves at all. 'Beauty enhanced, hearts restored' read the title of one disaster recovery brochure I picked up in Manila.

Determined that there must be money available somewhere, given the clear and overwhelming emergency needs, I continued my donor door-knocking and found myself invited to an unscheduled meeting that was described to me as 'something to do with the response'. Leaving no stone unturned, I showed up once more at the freezing steel and plate-glass towers of the diplomatic buildings in Manila and braced myself for another bout of hypothermia. I was ushered through the building to a small windowless office in which were seated a group of men in dark suits sitting around a conference table. Nobody looked up as I entered, and I took a seat to the side, unsure about the protocol in a room that had the sombre, formal and yet slightly edgy atmosphere of a yakuza conclave. Shortly after me the head of the UN in the Philippines arrived—a gregarious Brazilian woman who broke the monochrome uniformity of the room's inhabitants. She stared ahead and straightened her already immaculate hair before introducing herself and, continuing to address the middle distance, read from a prepared statement about the humanitarian catastrophe that Super Typhoon Bopha had caused. And as I looked around, following the direction of her gaze, I noticed that a large TV screen at the opposite end of the room had been turned on, displaying a cavernous room with what appeared to be a large number of people sitting at desks. It was clear that the proceedings were being broadcast. As my Brazilian colleague finished, she turned to me and asked if I would like to say anything. And with slowly dawning terror I realised, as the microphone made its way across the table to where I was sitting, that I was about to address the member states of the United Nations in session by videoconference from Manila.

But still the response lacked funds and without any kind of international institution systematically managing development and humanitarian funding, financial decisions were made in a way that was random, ad hoc and based on calculations of national interest rather than humanitarian needs. In this context, the Philippines ranked low and the dependency of humanitarian agencies on donor whims showed in their increasingly desperate attempts to attract attention. Everything was signposted and labelled: 'a gift of the American people', 'Canadian Aid', 'assistance from the European Commission'. Logos, brands and labels were everywhere despite the clear limits of the funding and the response, while donor institutions had gradually become more strident in the way they presented themselves. The formerly understated UK Department for International Development (DfID) had become the more aggressive UKAID, with the by-line 'from the British people' bizarrely tagged on hoardings outside the houses of grateful beneficiaries; the Australian Aid Agency embarrassingly flew the flag of a red kangaroo. It had become a criterion of funding for many donors that the 'beneficiaries' could state which country their assistance had come from. Some particularly ingratiating aid agencies printed special shirts for their staff to wear, which were decorated with the logos of all the donors—something that, as one colleague remarked, made them look like 'humanitarian racing drivers'.

When all else had largely failed, a 'donor mission' was organised in which representatives were invited to come and see the destruction caused by Typhoon Bopha for themselves. A small group of diplomats and aid agency representatives agreed and were flown around in helicopters from one destroyed village to the next to have a look. But they never really got close to anyone who had actually been affected—aid agencies had gone in paroxysms of sycophantic activity, printing more and more shirts for greater 'visibility' of their employees and even orchestrating distributions of food and relief items that happened to coincide with the donors' royal tour. Aid agency representatives hung around with funding proposals in their back pockets waiting for a moment when they could impress a donor with their new recovery concepts alluringly entitled 'Debris to shelter' or 'Ruins to resiliency'.

Security was also close. In one area, nearly a hundred families lived in a collapsed football stadium because they were unable to return to their original homes, which had been washed away in a vast torrent of sludge and rocks. The donor party was surrounded in concentric circles by their own heavily armed embassy security teams as well as the M16-toting Philippine Army Special Forces—much to the alarm of the unsuspecting families, who were engaged in such threatening activities as doing the washing, collecting water and preparing the evening meal. Whatever else, it was vital, as one UN colleague explained during a meeting, that no one used the donor visit as an 'opportunity to complain'.

Over dinner that night in the fake marble dining hall of a swanky hotel back in Davao, the donors declared themselves moved by the experience. The cash-strapped Spanish representative, remembering the good old days of Spain's dominion, pledged a paltry amount on the spot—as much as the dire conditions of the Spanish economy allowed. Other in-principle emergency pledges were made—still well short of the total amount needed.

'There seem to be a few people who need a house,' observed one of the more astute and generous representatives.

But the word 'emergency' as experienced by a villager in Mindanao and as understood in the fluoro-lit corridors and behind the office partitions of bureaucratic power in Canberra, Oslo, Brussels and Washington were clearly very different. Five months after the typhoon had hit, contracts were still being drawn up and funding criteria finalised. As we finished our reports late that evening, one of my colleagues looked up mournfully from his computer. 'I've been googling for half an hour and I can't find any good jokes about donor visits to underfunded disasters,' he said.

It was a strangely detached experience working to coordinate the humanitarian response. Overly zealous security restrictions meant that for the first few weeks we were unable to leave Davao, the main city of Mindanao—which had not been affected by the typhoon. The security rules were devised by someone who genuinely believed that we would be instantly captured and sold into captivity in order to fund the electoral aspirations of corrupt politicians. This was the fate suffered by an unfortunate Swiss birdwatcher, who had strayed, in hot pursuit of a rare and exotic 'twitch', into territory controlled by an insurgent group several thousand kilometres to the south.

We were stuck in an office overlooking the fake marble reception of an up-market hotel, where everything seemed like an elaborate and very earnest exercise rather than the real thing. We worked sixteen-hour days, seven days a week hunkered down in our office, attending meetings and gathering information remotely without actually seeing anything of the effects of the typhoon or talking to anyone who had first-hand experience. Below us, the crooner in the hotel restaurant played 'Born free' and the theme tune from *Superman* on his synthesiser.

After a week of being locked up, I decided I couldn't legitimately do any more without seeing for myself what had happened. As I finally drove out of Davao on a wet, grey morning, the devastation that I had been reading and meeting about was immediately apparent. Torrential rain had continued to cause massive flooding and, while the roads were at the high point, some villages lower in the valley were flooded up to roof level. By the sides of the road, men and women had constructed makeshift shelters with tarpaulins over the portable frames of string beds, piled high with family possessions, and occasionally articles for sale. The family rooster would be tethered at a high point nearby, out of danger.

Lining the highway out of town, stark evangelical bill-boards in black and white added an apocalyptic edge to the sense of catastrophe:

MY WAY IS THE HIGHWAY. —GOD

As we went on, it was clear that some aid had reached the people living in villages by the main roads, but it did not take much to find places that had received nothing. The floods and immensely strong winds had caused huge damage, and the landscape, under the grey clouds and incessant rain, evoked the Western Front in places—scarred earth, shattered trees and farms, the strewn wreckage of lives, homes and livelihoods across vast tracts of Southern Mindanao. The earth, deeply disturbed by years of mining and deforestation, had been churned by the typhoon. Where villages had stood, great mounds of mud, rock, and splintered wood remained.

Occasionally, as the rain stopped, the sound of chainsaws started as people began cutting up the debris and trying to re-make their homes. But these were few and far between—vast deforestation caused by the economic exploitation of Mindanao's famous hardwood trees had finally led to a government-imposed ban on chainsaws. But even those that were in circulation came at a cost. At about twenty cents per plank, the cost of wood was unaffordable to many of the tenant farmers who had lost everything. In the absence of an effectively funded aid effort, some people had started to build back using what resources they had. But for the majority, most were living in pathetic lean-tos made of the debris and rubble of their former homes. Rusty and bent corrugated-iron sheets had been carefully twisted back into shape and secured with stones and rope, while tarpaulins and bits of wood provided cover for families huddling in the rain amid the desolation of their destroyed farmland.

LOST? MY WAY IS YOUR ROADMAP. —GOD

And many lived by the side of the road because their land was still underwater. Hovels had sprung up alongside the main arterials—in some cases little more than tarpaulins wrapped around bed frames. In one 'spontaneous settlement' I entered, a well-meaning NGO had delivered a number of tents sent by a donor in the Middle East. Lightweight and made of non-waterproof canvas for arid climates, this 'aid' only made the situation worse.

Amid the chaos, destruction, and occasional signs of hope and reconstruction, I noticed again and again the neat, well-spaced triangular shelters in which the fighting cocks were kept. They were everything that, in many ways, the shelters provided during the relief effort were not. Understanding the territorial ego of the cockerels, the shelters were well-spaced, allowing for dignity, privacy and harmonious living. They were built on the high point of a hill and therefore not subject to flooding, and drainage trenches lined the huts in neat rows. Seed was scattered in designated areas to avoid crowding and confusion. In short, unlike the arrangements for humans, the arrangements for cocks met and even exceeded most humanitarian standards as set out in the field guides and handbooks of aid workers. But what these animals had, which many of their human counterparts clearly lacked, was an economic value.

FOLLOW ME.
—GOD

The god squad billboards listed a telephone number, and as we stalled in an intersection I rang up to find out whether the deity had any views on traffic congestion. A recorded message advised that the number was no longer attended.

With the flood waters receding, I decided to walk down from a ridge where World War II was commemorated by restaurants and plaster models of Japanese soldiers, and back through the streets choked with autorick-shaws and jeepneys belching diesel fumes. I walked past corner stores and retail outlets selling pirated DVDs, clothes and food; shops with names like Jolly Ant and Pot Dog. I walked on past the great malls of the city—upper-class malls and middle-class malls—and deep into the bridge-side slum where, clustered round a mosque, there were autorickshaw repair shops deep in oil, and clouds of dark soot from coconut husks being converted into charcoal. The upper- and middle-class malls were deeply aspirational: Western goods at Western prices and modelled by Europeans. The centrepiece of one mall, beneath a fashion boutique whose gothic script announced that it was called Bum, was a set of plastic European manniquins acting out the family ideal. A blond, muscular male manniquin stood over a reclining, bikini-clad female manniquin, while two blue-eyed plastic toddlers played with equally synthetic toys in a plastic-fantastic universe of fake beachside glamour. Further on, glass cabinets advertised Fairlane homes—designer pre-fabricated houses dominated by enormous garages where outsize models of American cars asserted that, in this miniaturised world, the occupants had arrived. A sleek young woman handed me a flyer. 'Fairlane Homes,' it said, 'moving to a better future.'

But if these malls were the new commercial and cultural centres of Philippine social life, then the cockfighting arena represented the brutal and bloody opposite end of the spectrum. The ice-cold synthetic paradise of the shopping centres gave way to the death, dust, beer and cigarettes of the cock pit. Walking past the Matina Gallera, a large, octagonal wooden building on the way down from the ridge, I heard a massive roar of noise. A barrage of sound—male voices in unison—erupted from the Gallera. As I got closer, the sound stopped. There was complete silence again as another bout started amid the deep concentration of men absorbed in a blood contest. It was a sport so important that wealthy politicians were known to fly their favourite beasts by Lear jet to major derbies. One international competition organised by American and Filipino enthusiasts was won by an estimable bird from Louisiana known as 'The Rapist'.

But what I assumed had been the roar of victory—the cockfighting equivalent of scoring a goal, a kill—was in fact the round of betting before the next fight. A sandpit stained with blood and covered in feathers stood at the centre of the Gallera, while advertisements for chook feed and rising politicians adorned the walls. Rising steeply on each side surrounding the pit were the packed stands, with special ringside seats for dignitaries. I took my seat at the back, in the 'gods' of the cockfighting world, peering down at the diminutive chickens below. Suddenly the roaring started again and the stadium erupted, everyone on their feet waving their hands and offering ten-fingered odds to everyone else in the stadium, attempting to find a series of betting partners who would offer compatible odds for opposing roosters in a kind of chook-centric version of traders on the floor of a stock exchange. Fearing that if I waved my hands around I might end up owing thousands of dollars to the rest of the crowd, I made a quiet bet with the man next to me—100 pesos for a large white rooster with an imposing manner against a smaller but potentially more agile darker bird.

The bout was almost over before it had begun. After the roosters were paraded for the betting public, they were then 'aggravated' by being held down while other roosters pecked at their heads. Once sufficiently annoyed, both roosters were placed on the sand and pushed encouragingly towards each other. The dark agile one moved immediately, leaping high above the head of its larger and more threatening foe and kicked back with its right leg in a single elegant leap. A five-inch stiletto razor (sharpened only at eclipses and the dark of the moon) attached to the rooster's heel sunk deep into its opponent's neck and the white bird, without having moved a step, sank lifelessly to the sand in an instant kill. The death of the rooster came as a shock, and I immediately regretted the bet that I had so cheerfully and unthinkingly entered into a few moments before.

The subsequent bouts were neither quick nor pretty. There was no majestic athleticism to the fight or the ritual of sporting bravery that provides a thin veneer to the brutality of blood sport. Following each round of crazed betting, more roosters would be 'tooled-up' with vicious spikes, tormented and set against each other in contests than usually resulted in a lethal stalemate in which both animals, hacked and bleeding, would collapse alongside each other only to picked up, roused and set against each other again. Outside the cock pit, trails of blood led to teams of men trying to stitch up wounded birds that could be repaired for breeding or to return to the ring again.

But there was more to the fights than the numbing succession of death and gore. As I left, crowds of beggars asked if I'd been successful with my betting and pointed to their stomachs for food. Inside, the betting, while complex, saw the exchange of small amounts of currency in minute bills folded many times so they could be kept between the thumb and forefinger of the right hand. It was, in a phrase of Jeremy Bentham, made famous by the anthropologist Clifford Geertz, an exercise in 'deep play'—a game in which the stakes were so high that no rational person would play it. They played nonetheless, because the deep play represented not only a need for cash by people who had little and in the typhoon had lost much, but a cultural interpretation of reality. Gone were the sanitised shopping malls. The tiered walls of the Matina Gallera were themselves a cyclonic formation around the still eye of the cock pit as the commotion of the betting formed a wall of sound around the death ritual at the centre. This was, in a way, an avian passion play in which the (known) outcome was less important than the performing of it.

In a country where newborns are carried until they are six months old because they are thought to be come not from the prosaic act of birth but descended the from the heavens, the cockfight is counter-reality, the experience that underpins, and is the frightening opposite of, the sterile aspirations of economic and social progress. As the crowd roared, pitiful amounts of money changed hands and, in the still of the storm, animals in a way more valuable than their owners fought to the end. The intensity of the betting, the socially hierarchical tiered stands and the concentration of the crowd during bursts of feathered fury stripped back the layers of interpretation, and began to merge in my imagination with the cyclonic churning of mud, stone, water and earth, where poor villages paid the ultimate price for being at the bottom the economic and status pyramid and thus at the front of the destructive social power of natural disasters.

CHAPTER 13:
THE SUFFERING IS THE STORY

DISSONANCE IS A FEATURE of humanitarian work—both in the field when international aid workers are dropped into emergencies in countries and during circumstances that are very different from the comfortable homes they have left, and when viewed from afar. Most of us are aware of emergencies and humanitarian crises through papers, the internet and television, and are confronted on an almost daily basis by the realistic, yet constructed, images of suffering in distant places. Generally, these are not images of the dead or those who have paid the ultimate price for the catastrophe that has engulfed them, but of the living. In the words of a French war correspondent, 'I think we have gone beyond the stage where it had to be the bodies and the blood. What is required today is suffering—particularly the suffering of women and children because it moves and mobilizes people more easily.' For some humanitarian workers, however, living amid the suffering can be almost the opposite. One of the most bizarre and disconnected moments I have witnessed was seeing the aid workers in Darfur watching Milan Fashion Week late in the evening on satellite TV—images of wealth, glamour and desirability that were the polar opposite of the locations in which we found ourselves. In some ways these oppositional images—suffering brought to stable domestic households on the evening news, or fashion shows beamed into an unstable desert war—reinforce the prevailing order. Aid workers can escape to a more glamorous reality via a short flight to consumerist civilization in London or Dubai (or even Milan), while the horrific nightly vision of suffering reminds viewers of the comfort of home and relative political and economic stability. Suffering prompts compassion and, as aid agencies hope, potential donations from an audience whose power to give funds for distant crises is itself a luxury.

We are moved, and often intentionally so, to sympathise with and assist as much as we can the 'survivors' whose 'stories' are briefly told—stories that make a claim for an entire life in a moment of suffering as if this is all that we need to know. Emergencies, taking aside for a moment the reality for those who experience them directly, can also be 'consumed'. It was no coincidence, as Susan Sontag observed, that Robert Capa's famous photograph in *Life* magazine of a Republican soldier in the Spanish civil war taken at the precise moment he was shot was positioned next to an advertisement for brilliantine with which an elegant city gent could slick his sophisticated hair.

Wars and crises draw the lens like nothing else, perhaps with the exception of sex. But in doing so, emergencies are presented in humanitarian terms. It is the life caught in the moment of suffering that becomes the 'story' and is often all that is told, or known, or thought necessary to know, about a given situation. It has become commonplace, for example, when seeking to understand what is happening in 'Africa' (as if the continent itself were a single country) to interview an aid worker. 'Africa'—the focus of so much of our contemporary images of suffering—becomes reduced to just that: a place whose history is a series of unconnected catastrophic dots whose totality, one is lead to believe, is history. This is the ultimate irony of working in crisis—the people whose stories are in fact history are those who cannot be helped. The dead cannot speak and we cannot know what they experienced, no matter how realistic the presentation of the crisis may be. The role of journalists and aid workers then becomes one of witnessing in difference ways—speaking for those who have died, representing the suffering of those who remain and interpreting, in messages designed to induce action, the meaning and response to these events.

This is a process that can be strange, especially for those not accustomed to media performance. While in the Philippines, I was asked for an interview by a Spanish TV crew who were covering the aftermath of Typhoon Bopha. While the majority of my work took place in government offices and meeting rooms trying to coordinate the response and help develop strategies for recovery, the TV crew had other ideas. They wanted images of action and for an hour I rehearsed with a colleague a series of made-up dialogues that featured us pointing at maps, moving pins, and posing in various stages of intense discussion. With the sound off, our improvised discussions turned to Spanish football and the relative merits of Barcelona verses Real Madrid, Lionel Messi against Ronaldo, while we simulated the frenetic activity of a relief command centre. In the end, only a thirty-second clip was used and clearly my acting skills needed improvement. Similarly, during a radio interview to describe the overall situation and give my observations from a recent field visit, I was asked by the interviewer what the public could do to help. At the time there were no appeals, and no organisations in Australia were taking public funds to support the Philippines response. The immediate answer, in short, was 'nothing', although this was not what I said. As I contemplated, with a sense of deflation, the reality of a media interview that did not end in an appeal for funds, it occurred to me that this had not been a waste of time. Rather, the absence of an appeal was part of something that I think is of longer-term importance, at least in the West—informed public discussion and understanding of history, politics and current events that is not necessarily reducible to an appeal for cash (useful as this is) or the manipulation of images of suffering.

Eglantyne Jebb, who founded the British NGO Save the Children in 1919, abandoned an earlier career as a teacher in part because of her dislike of children. 'I suppose it is a judgment on me for not caring about children that I am made to talk all day about the universal love of humanity toward them,' she wrote. She realised, however, that the suffering of children was one of the most powerful statements of vulnerability and apolitical humanitarian need—and, cynically, a brilliant marketing tool. Her 'starving baby' leaflets showing the dire conditions in post-war Germany were instrumental in raising funds and in changing commonly held attitudes that there should be no sympathy for the people of the country with which Britain had been at war. The idea that humanitarianism was beyond politics and cared for the defenceless was further reinforced by her supporter George Bernard Shaw, who famously wrote, 'I have no enemies under the age of seven'.

Images of children in crisis have remained the mainstay of the wider humanitarian 'pitch'. Depictions of such abject vulnerability demand immediate action and are imbued with moral, even parental, urgency. Children are not political, have limited agency, and strike at the heart of conceptions of family and community—a sense of empathy because everyone has, or at least once was, a child. They also raise money: a large number of NGOs, including World Vision and CARE, use images of children or some form of 'child sponsorship' to fund their broader operations under the logic that good development or humanitarian programs that assist a community will also benefit its younger members. How conflicts and disasters are witnessed domestically in the West through television and marketing campaigns is consequently a major and at times problematic component of humanitarian action itself—as ideas of innocent suffering and victimhood, in place of agency and local resourcefulness, are transposed onto societies in crisis. More specifically, organisations focusing on people who have not experienced picturesque suffering, such as the elderly, often struggle to raise sympathy and resources.

CHAPTER 14
PALAU

LEAVING THE PHILIPPINES, I headed straight for the Republic of Palau—a minute Pacific Island state a few hours' flight from Manila, which had also been hit by Typhoon Bopha. In contrast to the massive scale and energy of the Philippines with its megacities and huge extremes of wealth and poverty, Palau seemed to doze in a well-heeled Pacific torpor. Until 1994 Palau had been an American Pacific territory before signing a Compact of Free Association that granted it nominal independence in something resembling a condition of sovereign dependency on the United States. Prior to this Palau had been a German, then Japanese and, following World War II, an American territory. Influences of these multiple colonial masters lingered on. Palauans with names like Siegfried Nakamura hung out in well-chilled American diners musing over the gridiron with a Bud Light while being served by Filipina waitresses and kept afloat by US aid grants (including an additional $250 million to accommodate former Guantanamo Bay inmates from China's Uighur minority). In town, the most substantial-looking buildings were in fact Japanese air-raid shelters with metre-thick walls. On the adjacent island, the government of Taiwan had constructed an enormous replica of Washington DC's Capitol Hill in gratitude for diplomatic recognition. Shimmering white buildings arose from the surrounding paddock, crowned with domes and connected by sweeping colonnaded walkways that linked the legislature, the judiciary and the executive. Here a congress and a senate met while each of the sixteen state governors, answerable to their own state legislatures, had offices in the executive building—all for a total national population of around 20,000. Amazingly, in this relatively wealthy island-microcosm of the US, the civil service was run on a patronage basis, just like on the 'mainland'. The effective functions of government stopped every four years as one rent-seeking group of politically connected admin-istrators replaced another with each turn of the electoral cycle following campaigns that emphasised, in the slogan of one candidate, 'honor, family, military'.

In the morning, I went out with some volunteers to see what the typhoon had done to parts of Palau and how the recovery effort had gone. Nearly 100 houses had been destroyed along the coast, as well as many plantations. The government, with significant US backing, had the response in hand a few months after the typhoon hit. Most of the houses had been entirely reconstructed, with some argu-ments to be had about what colour they should be painted;

in contrast to the Philippines, where emergency assistance basically amounted to some tools and plastic sheets. It was hours before we saw our first house—not because these were far away, but because the route chosen circuitously passed a number of shops and gardens where the finest produce of Palau could be obtained in order to fuel our visit. Cans of Coke and sickly pineapple juice were stacked in the boot, while several roast chicken and fish dishes were ordered and collected. On the way, chocolates flowed and the volunteers munched on a bitter local berry mixed with a peculiar concoction of miso soup and KoolAid. Hitting a small speed hump, the driver turned to me and slurred through a mouth plugged with betel nut and tobacco, that the speed humps were enough exercise for the day.

It was quite the opposite to Typhoon Bopha as experienced in the Philippines. This was a well-funded response in a small but relatively prosperous society. Clearly no one was going to starve—the main complaint was that the three-bedroom houses being built by the government were sometimes too small, although painting them a light blue made them look bigger. There was no need here for cockfighting. In Palau, Budweiser, American football and occasional news of the typhoon broadcast on a flat-screen TV above the bar of the Pacific diner really did say it all.

CHAPTER 15
THE MICRO-STATES

I OPENED THE THROTTLE and tore down the tarmac, pushing a rusty motor scooter into the encroaching dusk as fast as it could go. The warm night air, thick with salt, flowed around me as the scooter cranked out its top speed and I headed for the edge of the island, to the sea. The atoll narrowed and the houses thinned and within a few minutes of what seemed like flight, I had arrived at a narrow isthmus on the Funafuti lagoon—a metre-wide strip of land that separated the moonlit mercury of the lagoon from the crashing waves of the great Pacific Ocean. In Tuvalu, one of the smallest countries on earth, the trip from end to end took a mere twenty minutes on a clapped-out motor scooter. But that short journey into the vast night of sky and ocean, sand and stars—a unity of the elements—made the Pacific so much greater than the sum of its micro-states. While during the day there was the risk of 'island fever'—a sense of being trapped forever on this minute coral atoll—at night, as everyone went to bed, the country seemed to expand with space and freedom and I urged my scooter faster, through the evening laughter, past the parliament buildings and the shanties at the edge of town and on, into the roar of the ocean and the sonorous grunting of the local pigs.

But this nocturnal freedom was confounded during the day. As the sun rose, Tuvalu's vulnerability was evident everywhere in this country where the highest point is around four metres above sea level, making it the second lowest country in the world (after the Maldives). Each year, during the king tides, a third of the island is submerged as water washes over the low-lying areas and bubbles up from below through the porous coral atoll. More alarming still, while Tuvalu is generally outside the cyclone belt, these are not completely unknown. The last cyclone, Bebe, which struck in 1972, caused the total inundation of Funafuti and destroyed all the island's buildings. When I arrived the climatic stress placed on Tuvalu by an unusually dry spell was immediately evident. Far from the lush tropical islands of Fiji or Tonga, Tuvalu seemed dry, hot and dusty. In the hotel there was only half an hour of water a day and reserves had been depleted to near catastrophic levels. As I travelled around the island the signs of drought were everywhere. Palm trees had turned brown and could no longer support their branches, which fell dying and discoloured all around.

As I walked around everything seemed in miniature. The Tuvalu Development Bank was a one-room building a few metres from the airport and the parliament building was a small open-sided meeting hall used by children to watch the arrival of the biweekly flights from Fiji. Nearby, a towering government administrative office, built by Taiwan in exchange for diplomatic recognition, was the only building more than two stories high on the atoll. There were other signs of Taiwanese influence—the hotel I stayed at was 'inaugurated by HE Hugh O'Young, Ambassador Extraordinary and Plenipotentiary of the Republic of China', and a small market garden project that sought to improve the Tuvaluan diet by introducing vegetables lined the runway. I wondered who Hugh O'Young was and if I would meet him, envisaging some washed-up old Chiang Kai-shek nationalist in a white suit who might emerge from behind one of the hotel's plastic palm trees.

The main feature of Funafuti was the runway. Built by the Americans during World War II it occupied the widest part of the island and, when not being used as an airstrip, was the focus of island life. Twice a week, the Tuvalu National Fire Truck would start its sirens and drive quickly up and down the landing strip to clear it of pedestrians, soccer players, and children gathered to watch the latest arrivals come in. For the rest of the week, however, the airstrip was the place to go to play soccer, to sit and talk with friends, to socialise and have fun, and—when the nights became too hot or people felt the need to escape from the pressures of living with their extended families, the airstrip was a place to sleep.

While the airstrip was the hub of social life, however, it had come at a cost. At either end of the runway, at the narrow tips of the croissant-shaped island, coral had been cut out of the atoll for rubble aggregate. This had left deep trenches at both ends, and as the population had gradually increased with migration from the outer islands, people had settled in the only land available to them—the trenches. Quickly these had filled with water and large communities had developed, living in shanties built over and around the trenches, which had also filled with rubbish in the absence of any waste disposal system. Every time there were heavy rains or strong winds severe damage was caused to the unstable houses in these areas. During drought, it was the opposite problem—the absence of water and the rubbish-strewn surrounds posed sanitation and hygiene risks from which people increasingly became ill. For all its charm even this miniature nation had its social dilemmas caused by 'development'.

A United Nations team had arrived on the same flight as me intending to show the Tuvalu government how it could use the latest Global Information Systems (GIS) to map the country's geography, topology and demographics from space. We sat in a small room with the UN team and representatives from Tuvalu's government and NGOs learning how to use the new software, each of us staring at our laptops as satellite images of atolls slowly came up on screen. In principal, it was a great idea—immediately available information that in larger countries could form an invaluable evidence base for a disaster response. But in Tuvalu, the global machinery of governance and technology reached its logical inconclusion and stumbled against the reality of a Pacific micro-state. Within minutes of everyone logging on to their computers simultaneously, the entire internet connection for the country was overloaded and none of the programs worked. While for a brief moment we could see Tuvalu from space, a short motor-scooter ride or even a twenty-minute walk would be able to reveal the realities on the ground in the event of a disaster. In any case, Tuvalu's problem was not sudden onset disasters like cyclones and tsunamis (although these were not entirely impossible) but drought, climate change and rising sea levels—things that were daily apparent even if the country's internet connection couldn't support more technologically complex ways of mapping them. Shortly after I had arrived in Tuvalu, a national emergency was declared because the island had literally run out of drinking water, and desalination plants had to be flown in from New Zealand and Australia to provide potable water for the 5000 people living on Funafuti.

If Tuvalu embodied the heroic, even titanic, struggle of small nation-states to be heard and to survive independently, Kiribati and some of the outer Cook Islands suggested a grimmer vision of the future. From the air, the prospect of arriving in Tarawa was breathtaking. After three hours' flight from Fiji over endless ocean, a small L-shaped atoll emerged in the distance and as we descended it resembled the fabled images of Pacific paradise. White sand beaches shaded with palm fronds lined the island, etched against the turquoise waters of the Tarawa lagoon—or at least so it seemed from thousands of feet in the air.

The reality, however, was very different. I soon found out that Tarawa, the main island of Kiribati, was one of the most densely populated places on earth, with a similar number of people per square kilometre to Beijing. Despite the country's total population being only 100,000 (in, if you include its water territories, an area greater than the size of Australia), most had migrated to Tarawa in search of jobs. The introduction of a money economy, combined with changes in occupation and lifestyle—pushed in part by the increasing difficulty, unpredictability and unfashionability of strenuous agricultural life growing yams and fishing on the outer islands—people had begun to concentrate in Tarawa. To accommodate them the government had begun to reclaim land, and a large number of the increasingly centralised population were now living in the Tarawa lagoon on land reclaimed with rubbish.

This concentration of people also brought other problems, particularly waste disposal. Traditionally, the ocean had been the great sanitiser of island life—with small populations and the vast currents of the Pacific waste, effluent and excreta had been instantly dissolved in seawater. But as the population had grown, the balance had shifted. The shallower waters of the lagoon were now so contaminated with sewage that we were under strict instructions not to eat fish for fear of contracting instant ciguatera poisoning. More alarmingly still, Kiribati was dependent for fresh water on rainfall that was stored in a water lens under the atoll, a layer of fresh water that sat above the heavier salt water of the ocean. Changes in sea level had begun to alter the balance of salt and fresh water in the lens, and the existing fresh water had become increasingly saline—a problem compounded by excessive water pumping from the additional population burden, and waste disposal directly into the fresh water lens itself. Despite Kiribati's idyllic appearance, the twin processes of 'development' and climate change had even led the president to put out a call for a new land (although this may have been an attempt to capture attention back from the Maldives, whose own president had started holding cabinet meetings underwater).

Another emblem of this process of change was the island of Mangaia in the Southern Group of the Cook Islands. At its height, the island had more than 2000 residents but these had now dwindled to a few hundred mainly elderly people. In the 1960s and '70s several New Zealand teachers made their way to Mangaia and started working in the local school. With talent and enthusiasm, the school quickly became one of the best in the country and educated successive generations of capable students. These students then promptly left for the main island of Rarotonga or for New Zealand as better job opportunities opened up and the hard life of cultivating taro and yam patches was made harder by rising sea levels, with salt water intruding into the soil. The pull of urban centres, development in the form of education, and regular flights between Mangaia and the capital now meant that those who remained were either too old or too sick to leave, or they remained on the island to maintain family properties.

The symbol of Mangaia was the adze—both an agricultural tool and an instrument of war, carved with an inverted Ж which was the stylistic representation of two brothers in battle. Outnumbered by the enemy, they tied themselves together with pandanus rope, back to back, and fought on against the odds with their stone adzes. The motif of struggle against the inevitable led to the use of the adze as a way to peace through sacrifice. When the Mangaia tribes fought, the side that thought it was about to lose would call a truce. A youth selected for ceremonial sacrifice would be dismembered with the adze and the remains distributed evenly to the island's villages as a sign that the dispute had been settled, if brutally—a sacrifice for the greater good.

But the symbol of the adze lived on even in more peaceful and depopulated times. I visited one woman who lived alone, surrounded by wall-to-wall pictures of family and friends, once from the island but now leading lives elsewhere. Moments of fun, excitement and merriment stared down in joyous but deafening silence on the one member of the family left behind: a moment in which the combined processes of development, climate change, and new economic opportunities were gradually starving the life of the island. There were children attending the school and elderly people tending to their taro patches, but the intervening generation had all but vanished, present only in the yellowing photos on the walls—the lives left behind had been figuratively adzed for the sake of future generations. In making the elderly stay behind, Mangaia's departed youth had reversed the cycle of history.

CHAPTER 16
THE IMPERIOUS CALL
OF HUMANITY AND
CIVILISATION

THE SOUTH SEAS and in particular Fiji, which I visited first, were strangely and remarkably familiar. Suva, Fiji's quaint colonial capital, held much of the charm of an English coastal village (although having later spent time on more remote Pacific islands, Suva would loom in the imagination as a kind of Pacific New York). Warm waves lapped a secluded harbour overlooked by the decaying grandeur of the Pacific Hotel and a nearby lawn bowls club. The centre was dominated by a large, brilliantly green maidan called Albert Park, while the street names echoed its imperial past as a distant yet loyal outpost of British rule. Victoria Parade intersected with Disraeli and Gladstone streets while boulevards named after colonial administrators and grand chiefs added to the town's diminutive yet stately appearance. Despite Fiji having become a republic, the Queen's head still featured on its banknotes and the Union Jack flew high in a proud corner of the baby-blue national flag. Neat rows of weatherboard houses with immaculate tropical gardens lined the harbour and the hilly streets around the capital remained resolute in their domestic ordinariness. At the far extremities of the town, new US and Chinese embassies had sprung up bristling with satellite dishes, antennae and barbed-wire fences while solid, squat yet ghostly white structures of the evangelising Mormon Church in the Pacific emerged as the latest player in the international conquest of souls just as the Americans and the Chinese increasingly sought dominance of the Pacific high seas.

But European trading and religious encounters with the Fijian islands had not started well. In the Fiji National Museum, alongside relics of great ocean-going canoes and intricate if dusty ancient carvings and woven baskets, was a small glass case celebrating the first missionary contact with Fiji. Inside was a Bible and a pair of spectacles belonging to the early Methodist missionary Thomas Baker, who had arrived in Fiji in the 1860s. In the case next to it was the pot and ceremonial fork with which he had been subsequently devoured—an extreme, if understandable, response to a cultural invasion that was only rectified in the 1990s as descendents of the Baker family and those of the local chief met to apologise in Fiji's by now deeply Methodist capital and, in a rather jovial encounter, they agreed not to do it again.

But the fuel of colonialism, religion and the newly

emerging politics of independent Fiji caused flickering tensions that undermined Fiji's cosy image as both a half-forgotten imperial outpost and a cheap tourist suntrap. In the words of the disenchanted National Fiji Party (a political party that represented Indian canegrowers who had arrived in Fiji in the nineteenth century as indentured labour):

Britain bequeathed the Westminster system of government to Fiji and it has worked ... since independence in spite of the lingering remains of an old feudal system: Government by the descendents of the Great Chiefs who clubbed and ate their way to power in these islands centuries ago.

But the role and importance of the 'Great Chiefs', while extremely important today, was itself a product of European, Indian and Fijian claims to cultural and political dominance—a fusion of tradition, invention and attempts to balance ethnic power in the colonies. It is often said of Fiji that its political turbulence is the product of competition between two particularly mismatched peoples—Fijians and Indo-Fijians—who are forced to cohabit a small set of islands while embodying mutually exclusive worlds. 'Even the prostitutes are ethnically divided,' I was told one night at Suva's Royal Yacht Club, where rusting brass sailing trophies and faded photographs of Europeans in evening dress lined the walls of the bar, aka the 'poop deck', an unimaginable social phenomenon in what was rapidly becoming, in parts, a South Pacific Ibiza.

Indo-Fijians, in this view, were the opposite of Fijians. A polytheistic community set against the evangelical monotheism of the islands, urban verses rural, Indian entrepreneurialism verses the Fijian status quo. Above all, disputes were about land and political power, with land as something that could be bought and sold and used for cash crops by Indians but seen as inalienable and collectively owned by Fijians. Indo-Fijians were increasingly perceived as a threat, initially by Europeans concerned that they may harbour links with India's own independence movements, and later by Fijians worried that an Indo-Fijian demographic advantage would translate into electoral power under the post-independence Westminster system. Fiji's 'coup culture' (two coups in 1987, another in 2000 and again in 2006) was in large part caused by the politics of ethnicity.

But if the political fault lines of modern Fiji were a product of a colonial legacy, so too were some of the country's main institutions and cultural concepts. The Grand Council of Chiefs, and the status attached to its members, was not an ancient assembly of 'big men'—it was established under colonial rule as a means, in part, of placating Fijians worried about the growing influence of recently arrived Indians. 'Traditional' Fijian values of *vanua*—collective ownership of land and ancestral connection to it—were equally recent. In this view, possession of land and traditions of indigenous government were conflated, and land came to refer to the more emotive concept of 'ancestral homeland' in which chiefs took on the role of perpetual custodians of Fijian identity, land and culture. This was an idea that was reinforced by the newly introduced religious enthusiasms of the Pacific. Christianity was fused onto the existing social order and chiefly hierarchies came to be seen as both the embodiment of cultural traditions and divinely ordained. The Fijian paramount chiefs came to believe that their authority had been directly handed down by God. The consequences of colonialism, conversion and migration from the subcontinent combined to change and entrench ethnicised perceptions of the political, economic and cultural sources of authority in Fiji.

'This used to be John Scott's house,' I was told over dinner one evening with some colleagues from the Red Cross. We had been taken to a large and imposing colonial mansion in Suva that had been converted into a Chinese-run restaurant advertising the nation's finest sizzling Angus steak. It was a deeply unfortunate historical irony, as I learned during the dinner while rapidly losing my interest in food—it had been the family home of a former head of the Fiji Red Cross, who had been killed with a cane knife along with his gay partner shortly after the military coup in 2000. This tragic and brutal murder also revealed the depth of change and social tension that lay behind the country's sunny facade.

The Scott family had arrived as Methodist missionaries in Fiji in the mid-1800s and had risen to prominence as jurists and colonial administrators in the century that followed, owning islands, hosting sunset cocktail parties on the balcony of the Pacific Hotel overlooking Suva Harbour, and receiving knighthoods and acclamations from the Queen on a royal tour of her palm-clad Pacific dominions. Theirs was a Pacific of the old colonial elite which, with its medals, uniforms, hierarchies and titles, saw itself a as modern European incarnation of the 'traditional' Fijian nobility that it had done so much to create both in and after its own image. The Scott family was the first to own a Rolls Royce in the country.

While most of the European residents, administrators

and traders left Fiji after independence in 1970, the Scott family, along with a handful of other European settler families, stayed on alternating between life in Fiji and careers in the UK and New Zealand. John Scott eventually returned permanently to Fiji as director of the Fiji Red Cross—an institution that, while serving the greater good, also closely replicated local social hierarchies. For this talented administrator and member of the much diminished European elite, the Fiji Red Cross provided an institution of both social status and influence that matched the family's traditional prominence in Fijian society. The annual Fiji Red Cross Ball was the social event and fundraiser of the year, where men in uniform and women in ball gowns and tiaras danced through the evening like colonial socialites, presided over by the country's new elite.

The military coup of 2000, led by Fijian ultra-nationalist and former army officer George Speight, was triggered by the election of Fiji's first Indian prime minister. The coup led the Red Cross and its director to play a direct and prominent humanitarian role. Using his personal standing and the mandated responsibilities of the Red Cross, John Scott became in many ways the media image of Fiji's political chaos. True to the Red Cross's mandate during conflict, he was able to cross the rebel lines surrounding parliament and deliver medical supplies and assistance to the parliamentarians locked inside. Wearing a white tabard with the Red Cross emblem on it, he was seen daily walking alone between the masked gunmen who surrounded the government buildings to assist and monitor the conditions of those inside—a nerve-wracking daily undertaking that was filmed and broadcast around the world, earning him the nickname 'angel of mercy'.

In other ways, however, John Scott and his partner stood out. Possibly still inhabiting the world of his parents and grandparents in which membership of the governing elite precluded censure, Scott was known for his good looks, wealthy lifestyle, and for being openly gay in a culturally conservative, evangelical Christian country that viewed homosexuality as a sin. Initially, the couple's murder was thought to have been a direct consequence of Scott's role during the coup, but the causes were deeper. Scott's gardener, a deeply devout but mentally unstable rugby player, had learned the evangelical lessons too well. He was possibly also gay and was thought to have had an affair with Scott, his partner or both of them. Seeing Scott again on television as the 'angel of mercy' seems to have fused a toxic mix of sex, sexuality and politics in an already unwell mind governed by an overzealous interpretation of Christian scripture. A few days after hacking his employers to death, the murderer turned himself in.

This story, told in the Scott family's former home (now restaurant) in Suva, seemed to capture both tragedy and change in Fiji. It was a lethal mix of postcolonial influences: ethnic politics, invented traditions and cultural confusion. The victim was a member of a European elite who may not have fully realised the days of untouchability were over in Fiji. The perpetrator, misguided by a set of religious, social and cultural norms that early European settlers and missionaries (including the Scott family) had brought to the Fiji islands was also, in some senses, a victim of the country's mutating politics and traditions.

The origins of humanitarian work are routinely attributed to a chance encounter between a famously moustachioed Swiss businessman, Henri Dunant (a sort of Florence Nightingale of the Red Cross Movement) and the combined forces of the Austro-Hungarian Empire, France and Sardinia at the battle of Solferino in 1859, in which more than 40,000 soldiers died or were injured in fifteen hours of semi-industrial carnage. In his book *A Memory of Solferino*, which is in many ways the foundational document of modern humanitarian work, Dunant begins by describing the pageantry and bravery of European aristocrats who, with true blue-blooded valour, charged into the thick of battle at the head of suicidally loyal troops, only to enjoy a convivial dinner with each other in the evening. In a little-quoted footnote, Dunant describes a merry après-slaughter scene in which the victorious French and defeated Austrian generals reminisce over a few bottles of Châteauneuf-du-Pape in the company of the Sardinian King Vittorio Emmanuele (future monarch of a united Italy).

> *"Now that you are friends" said the King laughing "sit side by side and talk". The generals could now ask one another about the details of the battle. One look at the Austrian General's loyal smile was enough evidence that all the bitterness was over. As for the French General, we all know that he had no reason for feeling any. Such is war; such is the life of a soldier. These two generals who were so friendly that autumn, will perhaps be fighting each other again next year, and then dine again together somewhere the year following!*

What saves Dunant's in many ways boy scout–like account of one of the most terrible battles of its day, however, is a keen appreciation of its horror. While it has the typical array of gallant uniforms, blaring trumpets, glorious changes and heroic last stands around the sacred regimental flag, the book is also a graphic account of mass killing. Uniquely, the shocking descriptions of slaughter to which the non-aristocratic soldiery were subjected do not end on the battlefield. By far the worst are kept for accounts of the operating theatre before the days of anaesthetic. In a description that captures some of the growing professionalism of medicine as well as its intense brutality and frequent incompetence, *A Memory of Solferino* includes this harrowing amputation scene for a broken leg that had become gangrenous.

The surgeon began to separate the skin from the muscles under it … Then he cut the away the flesh from the skin and raised the skin about an inch, like a sort of cuff … and with a vigorous movement cut right through the muscles with his knife, as far as the bone. A torrent of blood burst from the arteries, covering the surgeon and dripping on to the floor … The orderly had little experience and did not know how to stop the haemorrhage by applying his thumb to the blood vessels in the right way … It was now indeed time for the saw, and I could hear the grating of the steel as it entered the living bone and separated the half-rotten limb from the body.

Also crucial to the account is the observation that wars did not only involve soldiers but civilians and social institutions as well. Expressing horror at the way the killing continued in churches, where fleeing enemy soldiers sought refuge behind an altar, despite the church's weak promise of protection as a 'house of peace', Dunant concluded that some people and places should be internationally recognised as *hors de combat*—'out of the fight'. These included prisoners of war, the injured, medical orderlies, hospitals and cultural institutions such as churches that, nominally at least, offered protection. More important still was Dunant's observation of the roles played by civilians, especially women, in providing aid, assistance, medical support, food, shelter and basic life-saving humanitarian necessities to the pathetic remains of people who, only a few hours before, had been able-bodied soldiers—irrespective of which side they had fought on. These civilian volunteers formed spontaneous aid committees and provided, with few resources and little experience, the relief services that the armies themselves did not provide and did so instinctively, without discrimination the basis of the soldiers' origins. Despite the best of intentions, qualified help was rare:

> *Oh how valuable it would have been … to have a hundred experienced and qualified voluntary orderlies and nurses. Such a group would have formed a nucleus around which could have been rallied the scanty help and dispersed efforts which needed competent guidance … most of those who brought their own goodwill to the task lacked the necessary knowledge and experience, so that their efforts were inadequate and often ineffective.*

While witnessing the event, Dunant himself strove to do as much as his background in the Swiss banking industry allowed him—the provision of bandages, cigars and pipes to wounded soldiers whose thick fug of burning tobacco would, he hoped, restore calm and hide the stench of rotting flesh. However effective his own interventions might have been, the broader lessons had been learnt. *A Memory of Solferino* called for a convention 'inviolate in character', which would form the basis for societies devoted to the relief of the wounded in wartime. 'Humanity and civilization,' Dunant wrote, 'call imperiously for such an organization'. Strikingly, the appeal was made not just to the European aristocracy, but universally: to people of 'all countries and all classes ... to ladies as well as men'. It was an appeal for the creation of a humanitarian agency made to 'every nation, every district, and every family, since no man can say with certainty that he is forever safe from the possibility of war'. The result was the signing of the First Geneva Convention 'for the amelioration of the wounded in armies in the field' by all twelve European heads of state in 1864 and the establishment of the International Committee of the Red Cross (ICRC) as the professional relief service, along with country-specific Red Cross societies that would form the civilian volunteer base needed for relief work.

But the 'imperious call' of humanity and civilisation was heard not only by Dunant and the founders of the Red Cross Movement but by individuals, organisations and states that have variously interpreted what the terms 'humanity' and 'civilisation' actually are, and the means by which they might be achieved. Where the Red Cross sought to limit the destructive power of war, the professionalisation of military medicine and nursing was already well underway through the efforts of Florence Nightingale during the Crimean War, between 1853 and 1856. While Dunant had admired Nightingale and acknowledged her as one the inspirations behind the founding of the Red Cross, Nightingale was more sceptical. In her view, such an organisation would only ease the responsibility for, and cost of, the care of wounded soldiers on war ministries and would paradoxically encourage them to go to war.

A prime motivation for nineteenth-century charitable societies was the concept of the 'deserving poor', who could be both materially aided and brought into the Christian fold. In 1865 another ostensibly humanitarian international institution was established, this time combining religious obscurantism with military hierarchy: the Salvation Army. The 1865 motto under which these soldiers of salvation marched was the 'three Ss' that would be delivered to the 'down-and-outs'—'soup, soap, and salvation'. The Salvation Army's founder, 'General' William Booth, inverted the then current conceptions about the Dark Continent (Africa) and applied them to the newly industrialised society of mid-nineteenth-century England in his book *Darkest England and the Way Out*. Applying the imperial concept of the 'civilizing mission' to parts of England itself, Booth observed that intense poverty, alcoholism and generally heathen behaviour existed in equal measure in England as it did in Africa. He formed his 'army' in order to deliver 'mankind from misery, either in this world or the next' and to facilitate the 'regeneration or remaking of the individual by the power of the Holy Ghost through Jesus Christ'. When discussing the need for a volunteer army to tackle poverty and irreligion at the heart of the imperial metropolis itself, Booth is said to have cried: 'I'm not a volunteer, I'm a regular soldier'.

William Booth's concept of a Salvation Army ministering

to the urban poor was a domestic version of what would become a greater ideological justification for imperial rule and even expansion, especially in the 1890s 'scramble for Africa'. Empires were expanding beyond their role as essentially state-backed private companies, such as the British East India Company, which was motivated by the incentive of monopoly profits rather than by the idea of good governance or 'saving souls'. This coincided with a rise in evangelical Christianity and, at least in theory, a rejection of outright commercialism and Christian pietism. In this new, 'muscular' form of evangelical endeavour, the role of the state was central in realising the practical ambitions of conquest and conversion as well as the notion that religious truth could be found through 'good works'. In this context the idea that 'trade followed the flag', and that the flag represented liberal rule and moral progress, underpinned the imperial ideal of the 'civilising mission'—variously represented in France, Britain and the United States as 'white man's burden' and Manifest Destiny. For Cecil Rhodes, the arch-imperial mining magnate and South African politician whose Rhodes scholarships sought to create a ruling imperial elite who would combine scholarly and sporting achievement with moral force, 'colonialism is philanthropy plus five per cent'.

This ethical revolution caused the ire of Karl Marx, who was the first to see the interconnection between a newly moralising culture and massive economic change. In the context of rapid industrialisation in the nineteenth century, Marx wrote in the *Communist Manifesto* that such charitable organisations served only to oil the wheels of capitalist excess—the humanitarian impulse was more about the increasingly urgent need to maintain social stability and the economic order than it was about philanthropy. These individuals and institutions were 'economists, philanthropists, humanitarians, improvers of the condition of the working class, organisers of charity, members of societies for the prevention of cruelty to animals, temperance fanatics, hole-and-corner reformers of every imaginable kind'.

In a recent interview with the Australian Broadcasting Corporation, billionaire philanthropist Bill Gates (whose foundation, courtesy of Microsoft millions and Warren Buffet's fortune, is among the largest charitable institutions in the world) remarked that he left the 'easy' tasks to government but thought that private organisations such as his were best placed to address the really challenging issues of our day—education, health and family planning. The foundation is best known for its investment in research into and prevention of polio and malaria, as well as its attempts to tackle the global HIV epidemic. Gates pointed out the flexibility of the funding to pursue new and innovative solutions, and cited a competition to find out which sort of condom produced the most sexual pleasure. Indeed, it is difficult to imagine the more stolid donor institutions relying on taxpayer funding to invest in condom research for fear, if nothing else, of conservative political backlash. Gates may be widely lauded but his view, in which the arms of government are privatised, is a troubling one (not to mention that he might make a more substantial contribution to health and education were Microsoft to pay appropriate tax within his own country).

The problem is essentially twofold. At a mysterious

meeting of major US philanthropists, The Giving Pledge, sixty-nine of these philanthropists committed to giving away 50 per cent of their fortunes: a total estimated amount of $125 billion, more than ten times the total United Nations operating budget. No matter how much 'good' such wealthy individuals have done, who are they to make decisions for and on behalf of millions of others, solely on the basis of their private wealth? Also problematic is the idea that these funds can be used more effectively to address complex problems, leaving the world's 'easy' issues to governments and governmental institutions such as the UN. Regardless of the success of polio vaccination programs, for example, it is extraordinarily naive, even arrogant, to assume that fundamental issues of war and peace, governance in developing countries, complex responses to climate change, the development of stable democracies and so on are the 'simple' tasks. The invidious nature of what Gates is proposing is that technocratic solutions to technocratically solvable problems can address fundamental questions of social, economic and political justice, while at the same time withholding funds (through tax minimisation) from government institutions that have a democratic mandate and responsibility for such challenges. What is important, if humanitarian issues are to be effectively managed in the future, is that this management occurs through democratically mandated and accountable governments whose influence and power goes well beyond the mere disbursement of cash. And this process, in our neo-conservative age, begins with education about the ideals and achievements of the United Nations and social democracies.

In one stark example, noted by Amartya Sen, the

complex problem of famine in India—which caused more than 1.5 million deaths in 1943—has not recurred in the post-independence period precisely because of the existence of a social democracy that is responsive to the needs, vulnerabilities and concerns of voters. Despite earning significantly less income per capita than their counterparts in the US, the citizens of the south Indian state of Kerala actually live longer precisely because of the maximisation, if not of wealth, then at least of opportunity as a result of successive government policies in response to the exigencies of electoral politics. It is this reform that is needed to address development and humanitarian challenges rather than the privatisation of compassion.

CHAPTER 17
TSUNAMI IN A TIN CAN

AT 06:48 ON 1 OCTOBER 2009 an underwater earthquake off the coast of Samoa caused a massive and fast-moving displacement of water that, fifteen minutes later, slammed into the palm-fronded coastal villages of Southern Upolu—the tourist heart of Samoa's main island. One hundred and forty-nine people were crushed or drowned and more the 5000 people were affected by waves that, owing to the towering cliffs overlooking the village of Lalomanu, reached up to 15 metres high.

Footage emerged of the vast tsunami waves sweeping across the beach fronts from Western and American Samoa, smashing houses and lifting cars like children's toys in a bathtub. The image of one of the happy isles of Oceania pounded by what was presented as a random act of unstoppable natural brutality resonated vividly with images of the

2001 Asian tsunami and hit a tourist nerve. The Samoa tsunami, as it became known, connected with a the global nexus of beach culture, cheap resorts, and holidays in the sun. In addition to loss of life and destruction of property, the tsunami was presented as a 'coconut catastrophe' that sent shock waves through tourist hubs from the Pacific to Thailand and the Costa del Sol.

The island of Niuatoputapu, aka Tin Can Island, 300 kilometres from the earthquake's epicentre and not part of Samoa but of the Kingdom of Tonga, did not belong to this nexus of almost fashionable beachside disaster locations.

Surrounded by an almost impenetrable reef, Niuatoputapu was in the distant north of the Tongan archipelago—more than three hours' flight away from the central island hub of Vava'u in a specially chartered Chathams Pacific Islander. Before it sank in Tonga's worst disaster, the ageing and unseaworthy *Princess Ashika* had taken over two weeks of chundrous chugging across open seas to get there. Unable to get near the island because of the reef, the *Ashika* had lowered passengers and supplies into smaller motorboats, which then made their way back to the island through an especially cut corridor in the reef. In this way, the island's staples of huge vats of expired Salisbury corned beef, tuna, packet noodles, damp cardboard cylinders of stale Pringles, and assorted Arnott's digestive and chocolate biscuits were imported.

Despite this, the island managed to maintain a population of 800 people, clustered in small hamlets along the seafront—Hihifo, Vaipoa, Falehau and Tafahi. All were rubble by the time I arrived almost three weeks after the tsunami, sent to assess options for the 'early recovery' programs. The imprint of leftover normality lingered on in the abandoned furniture, the cleared paths and the rubble-strewn outline of where houses had been.

I had arrived for the first time in Tonga almost a year before and had slowly travelled through the islands of Tongatapu, Vava'u and Ha'apai. The Kingdom was quite different from anywhere else I had been in the Pacific and this became immediately apparent when I landed at the airport unknowingly on the same flight as a member of the royal family. As we touched down, a military brass band dressed in red coats and brilliant white plumed pith helmets marched up and down the tarmac playing the national anthem before being left behind by the VIP's jeep, bearing an enormous royal standard, which took off down Tongatapu's one road surrounded by motorcycle outriders.

It was a bizarre beginning. The local organisation I worked for, being in many senses a creature of the establishment, was linked intricately with the peculiarities of Tongan monarchic patronage. At the office, ancient staff members wandered in and out, their irrevocable positions owed to long-defunct royal command. A giant carved hat stand, which once held pride of place in the palace bedroom, stood in the central corridor of the organisation—a hindrance to all but an almost untouchable totem of regal favour.

The obscurity and idiosyncrasy of the Tongan political system was a reflection of an extreme form of Polynesian hierarchy (also evident in chiefdom structures of Samoa and pre-colonial Hawai'i) and the country's unique position as the only Pacific nation—in a still deeply colonial region—to escape imperial subjugation. While it had been informally a British protectorate, the traditional independence of Tonga had nonetheless led to an absorption of the style and substance of British nineteenth-century politics. Tonga had the region's first written constitution—that superimposed a Westminster system of government (along with prime minister, cabinet, legislature and judiciary) but which actually strengthened indigenous political structures by constitutionally enshrining the legal, property and political rights of the monarchy and the landed nobility. The lords of thirty politically significant families had the right to govern.

In style, the Tongan political system also appeared odd with its insistence on traditional clothes, and elaborate nineteenth-century military uniforms netted in braid, coloured sashes and the pomp and circumstance of the British Raj, miniaturised and transported to the small Pacific island. But this too was a piece of political theatre designed to reinforce the concept of what anthropologists have called the 'domesticated stranger king'.

In Tonga there are no migration myths, unlike much of the rest of the region. Instead, the earliest foundation stories talk of the inhabitants of the main island, Tongatapu, as 'small, black and descended from worms'. Other foundation stories suggested that early rulers had 'descended from the skies' following the union of a divine father with a Tongan mother. The fusion of these stories suggested at some stage an invading ruler had cleverly combined elements of both the myth of divine origins while also suggesting that the monarchy was an integral part of indigenous society—hence being descended from worms.

Seen in this context, the apparent incongruity of the miniature Raj of the Pacific—of ermine-clad nobles and

Sandhurst-educated, monocle-sporting kings, separated from each other and from the constitutionally enshrined 'commoner' class by wealth, power and even distinct dialects—began to appear marginally less unreal. These anomalous traditions had been coopted by an indigenous hierarchy seeking to retain power and influence. The Tongans had understood and adapted to the Pacific the lessons of Frederick the Great in Prussia: reform from above before you are reformed from below.

On the final evening of my Tongan visit, I again saw the royal cavalcade—this time halted outside a small house whose entrance was guarded by brass canon. I stopped to watch and after a few minutes was rewarded as an enormous man wobbled along a red carpet at a stately pace from the house to the royal car as his guards stood to attention and saluted. He got in but the door remained open and the guards stood frozen at attention. Some minutes passed before a minute dog bounded out of the house and leapt into the car and in a second the door slammed, the outriders ripped their motorbike throttles and the cavalcade surged powerfully onto the road forcing the passing traffic onto an embankment, their majesties large and small progressing imperially home beneath the fluttering royal standard, leaving behind the roar, a tail of dust and the gentle lapping of the Pacific shore.

My second visit to Tonga was altogether grimmer. While the world's eyes had been fixed on Samoa, higher waves with greater force had flattened three of the four hamlets of Niuatoputapu. Many had been caught in waves up to 17 metres high and nine people had died—a catastrophic loss on an island of only 800 people. Unlike in Samoa, where some had received a tsunami warning—15 minutes till impact—there was no warning in Niua. People I spoke to said they had felt a light tremor, but that this was no different to previous tremors except that it had lasted almost ten minutes. Minutes after that the first of three increasingly large waves struck.

I flew in an antique Douglas DC-3—described as a collection of parts flying in loose formation—to the Northern Island of Vava'u and then transferred to a mosquito-like Islander for the three-hour journey to Niuatoputapu. On the tarmac, as we loaded up, there was a delay—to maintain balance, the eight passengers had to be reseated in order to make way for a colossal noble who by birthright and in order to distribute his weight had to be placed by himself on an even keel at the back of the plane. I was the loser in this readjustment and was crammed in at the front between the pilot and the Permanent Secretary to the Cabinet—a man named Busby—who during the flight and almost incomprehensibly above the roar of the propeller described the World Bank's Niua reconstruction plan: 150 Californian bungalows to be constructed in neat rows at vast expense from imported brick and concrete on an inaccessible island without a port in the middle of the Pacific Ocean.

The village of Hihifo was the worst hit and there was nothing left standing except the shell of someone's lovingly constructed blue-tiled concrete bathroom—standing alone now, without a roof or attached house, overlooking the sea. The rest was rubble: bricks, concrete, and hideously twisted sheets of corrugated iron. The pulverised remains of a car sat on top of what was once a roof but had now been smashed out of recognition and lay on the ground. Through the rubble and debris a road and some paths had been cleared by a New Zealand navy unit sent up from Tongatapu. The ship was too big to land and the navy had to create a helicopter airbridge to the island in order to deliver supplies and help in the clean-up. Near the entrance to the village, a slightly battered community noticeboard still stood and, in a malapropism that had turned into an apocalyptic temptation of fate, the sign read (CLEAN):

Community
Leader
Eradication
Around
Niuatoputapu

Strangely, amid the wreckage of the tsunami, I suddenly felt almost at home. Far from being the shock they had once been, disasters had become an almost familiar scene—the constant accompaniment, however grim and destructive, of human settlement and construction. And in this place, so different from my own, this destruction, the entire reason for my visit, was also a point of connection. Fortunately, while the villages had been destroyed the agricultural land was at a higher altitude and remained untouched. Everyone had moved from the villages to their gardens and were living in shanties and tents. What had gone, however, were the food stocks, and the water wells near the coast had been contaminated with salt water. Beyond the digestive biscuits, stale chocolates and tinned beef at the one remaining general store, there was almost nothing to eat and very little to drink. We slept on the floor of the local school and ate one meal a day—boiled rice mixed with tinned beef and cooked over an open fire made of broken pieces of people's former homes. In the dry heat of the day, as I walked between the villages comparing the elaborate reconstruction plans with the more practical concerns of recovery—shelter and water—a small party of children followed this strange, pale foreigner through the rubble. They clearly had taken pity on my wanderings and had each brought delicious, refreshing gifts. And so I found myself moments later standing in the sun, on my own, the proud possessor of half a dozen watermelons—extravagant gifts in a context of food and water shortage for a total stranger from a people whose island lives had been shattered only a few short weeks before.

In the ruins of what had been the local bank branch, situated next to a twisted wreck of metal that was all that remained of the island's satellite dish, I met the bank manager and we talked, sitting on a stray block of concrete. She had been at home but was alerted by shouts that 'the sea is coming' and went outside to the ground wet and pigs running around in mad confusion—clearly the result of a large wave. Getting in her van to drive down to the shore, she suddenly saw a second wave:

surging up ashore behind the bank, and then an even larger wave beyond that a few hundred metres away. This wave was higher than the coconut trees and I felt a surge of panic and began reversing up the road. By this time, people had jumped into the back of my van, onto the roof too, and others were clinging to the sides, standing on the running board. I was keeping an eye on the larger wave all the time, which by now had lifted and was floating an entire house towards us.

Another survivor described how he had left home early in the morning to go fishing and had felt the earthquake as he returned with his catch. Turning around, he saw the sea surging over the reef where he had just been. He climbed a tree just in time because a second wave crashed through the village and watched helpless as bits of debris from his house floated past. Eventually the sea receded and he climbed down to find that there 'was nothing left at all, and it was much the same for the village, nothing but wreckage, and fish flapping on the ground'.

On the way back, we stopped at the island of Vava'u awaiting a connecting flight back to Tongatapu. After Niuatoputapu's dry heat, destruction, solemnity and the incredible generosity of its people, 'normality' in the tourist centre of Vava'u was bizarre, and my Tongan colleague Iengi and I felt equally out of place. 'These strange foreigners,' Iengi muttered to me under his breath as we watch a group of international yachting families dressed up for Halloween—and it took me a second to remember that I was a foreigner too.

PART 4
KAZAN, 1999

STUDENT DAYS: COUNTING THE COST OF POST-SOVIET STATE COLLAPSE

CHAPTER 18
SEARCHING FOR 'THE DOMES'

ENCLOSED IN THE OBSIDIAN blackness of a Russian winter's night, the Krasnoyarsk Express had come to an unscheduled stop. In the last carriage—'hard class'—passengers began to stir. I peered over the edge of my steel bunk, dazed and dimly aware that we had not yet arrived. There were people silently milling around outside, connected somehow to swiftly moving sparks of light. The carriage door opened, refreshing us all with a trans-Caucasian frost and a man entered, walking with arctic slowness through the carriage carrying a chandelier, followed by another chandelier-carrier and another. Chandeliers of all cuts, sizes and varieties—for grand drawing rooms of the people or modest workers' apartments—the glinting high-Soviet procession of cut glass paraded in silence past the barely conscious inhabitants of hard class and out again into the night. And as they went, the Krasnoyarsk Express resumed our journey eastward to Kazan.

It was 1999, a decade after the fall of the Berlin Wall, six years after the dismemberment of the post-Soviet Commonwealth of Independent States, and Russia was still groaning in transition. In this place, Vladimir Putin resurrected Stalin's national anthem (minus references to the USSR and the 'Party of Lenin'). Isaac Rosenbaum, a former underground chanteur, revived ballads from the Soviet Union's last colonial misadventure in Afghanistan and sang with confusedly heartfelt historical anachronism: 'I'm from St Petersburg, Russia, USSR'. Camp boy bands—like Ivanushki International—also vied for the public's affection by lip-synching anodyne schmaltz-pop before stiff rows of teenagers unsure of how to respond to their new musical freedom but desperately wanting to be fashionable in the New Russia. Leninism, great-Russian chauvinism, authoritarianism and plastic consumerism commingled toxically along with the horrendous human cost of state collapse.

I had arrived in Russia in search of a language school to teach English and a university to learn Russian. I had an email from someone in Kazan—'come', it had said, 'we'll offer you $450 a month'—and Kazan sounded good. I knew that in Moscow the train stations were built in the predominant architectural style of their destination. Thus Finland station, where Lenin had returned to Russia in a sealed train from Germany in 1917, had a light Scandinavian simplicity. Yaroslavl station's spires echoed the Huon pine settlements of Siberia and the Far East. Kazan station—the jewel—was all dark cavernous interiors of polished marble and celestially brilliant onion domes, an iconic fusion of Byzantine Orthodoxy and Islam. And after arriving at Moscow's Sheremetyevo airport I headed straight for the domes.

I had no address, no phone number, and knew nothing about Kazan beyond its exotic name. I had been employed, if that is the right word, by a grandly named organisation called Linguamir (a Russian play on the words for language, world and peace)—which also styled itself as the Volga Centre for Education and Information. Before I arrived, there had been a debate about whether to rename Linguamir with the more aspirational and less Soviet-sounding appellation Win Brand: a short, pugnacious and avaricious phrase deemed more appropriate to the New Russia. I had been given the job title *prepodavatsil*—a word roughly equivalent to 'professor' in the general sense of one who teaches adults—which appeared to inspire a mildly dutiful respect among the lower echelons of the post-Soviet bureaucracy and the occasional salute from the paramilitary police.

Knowing no Russian, and unable to read the Cyrillic script, I soon became hopelessly lost in the vast lugubrious railway mausoleum of Kazan station. The language section of my guide book—before I lost it—under the heading 'Useful Phrases' provided long polysyllabic agglutinations that were totally unpronounceable. While I briefly held it upside down, in a futile search for greater clarity, a young Russian couple took pity on me. They helped me change my money and buy my ticket before introducing me to an Italian-speaking Russian, incongruously named Olympia, who they identified by her 'Western clothes'. While I knew no Italian it was close enough to English, after being so woefully lost in Russian, that I felt I could breathe in my own language again. Somehow Olympia guided me to my platform, train and carriage. I waved as she left, waiting for a train back to Ukraine and her job at an almost totally obsolete car factory to resume production of Ukraine's national automobile, the Zhiguli (equivalent to the Russian Lada or the East German Trabant)—a leaky, cast-iron fridge on wheels and an industrial dinosaur doomed in a world without command economies or production quotas.

In Kazan I knew no one. From the station, I dragged my bags down the main street—Bauman Street—a solidly bourgeois nineteenth-century promenade with ornate streetlights and balustraded buildings. It was cold and clear and I wanted to find an internet cafe where I could email my contact to say I'd arrived. A Turkish kebab seller directed me to the Hotel Tatarstan—a drab Soviet concrete block— and I found myself in a brown room with brown stuccoed walls and a hard bed with a severely tucked brown polyester blanket. It was a drab and awful world that smelled of cigarettes and air-freshener and was relieved only by the dull grey of a steel chair in the corner. It gave the impression of only recently having been vacated by members of the Politbureau in pre-lapsarian Soviet days. I dumped my bags and escaped quickly back out to the street—bare now in the looming twilight, a few people walking in black overcoats and oversized fur hats as they made their penumbral way home.

I walked on, past the closing shops and the disappearing crowds, stopping random strangers with incomprehensible English requests for directions. One man pointed to an ancient and derelict building—it had the look of a nine-teenth-century Grand Hotel but had fallen on a century of hard times. Painted green, its once magnificent awnings were in an advanced state of decay, and noble columns upheld by muscle-bound caryatids sagged alarmingly. Not only were these forgotten gods banished by the revolution but they had been condemned to crushing indifference and prolonged neglect. Architecturally, they were a futile attempt to prop up a long defunct tsarist political order whose vestigial memory lingered on in the collapsing masonry of the present.

I made for what would once have been the grand entrance to the Hotel Kazan, but found the doors locked and a small ripped cardboard sign with an arrow that pointed to a side entrance. I walked on, through a gap in the corrugated-iron fence, and followed a path being cleared by a platoon of grey-coated Russian Army conscripts who, more or less as I arrived, decided to take a urinal break and started pissing against the walls leading up the hotel's makeshift entrance. Inside, I was immediately struck by the fetid air, the damp red carpet, and an immense spiral staircase whose luminescent marble steps wove their way funereally up into the gloom.

Up I walked, and on the second floor found an ancient Intourist office—formerly the official chaperone of any foreign visitor, but now reduced to a redundant bureaucratic outpost—and a man inside it who spoke German. This was at least more comprehensible to me than Russian and he intoned sagely and pointed his finger ominously upward towards the staircase. I climbed higher, losing confidence with every step and beginning to think my Russian adventure was about to be pathetically extinguished in the musty, cloying air of the disgusting Hotel Kazan. I followed yet another dank corridor, and at the end as it turned almost to total darkness I noticed a large steel door that was slightly ajar. I opened it cautiously and in the relative glare of a lighted room, I made out two young Tatar women.

'Tom—you've arrived! Welcome to Kazan.'

It was dark and cold and I desperately wanted a warm room and food. But in the excitement of my arrival, my new colleagues had decided to take me to meet their friends and to go on a nocturnal tour of the city. I was introduced to Misha—a silent, calm architecture student with hooded blue eyes. As we laboured over conversation I asked what he enjoyed about university. 'Specialist military training,' he replied and, after a long pause, 'I am sniper.'

Soviet stereotypes seemed to live on in modern Kazan. The leader of our party, Natasha—tall, powerfully built with waist-length blond hair—was herself something of a human version of the iconic statues of muscle-bound 'Soviet woman' breaking free of their capitalist chains. 'To Victory Square, he must learn about Russia!' she cried and we followed. I warmed immediately to my two Tatar colleagues—Zulfyia and Albina—as we sat shivering in the back of Natasha's ancient Lada rumbling at speed through the backstreets of Kazan, guided with ballistic precision by Misha. Like me, the last thing on their minds on that freezing night appeared to be rusting Soviet military hardware.

Natasha was an aeronautical engineer but in the post-Soviet collapse found herself out of work designing jet fighters and, for $50 a month, had become the language school administrator. Her Russia was turbocharged, and the encroaching winter and steady sleet provided no disincentive to the worship of the once glorious Russian military machine on display at Victory Square—a gigantic wrecking yard of Tupolevs, Illyushins, and MiG fighters. The tour became a whirlwind of air-speed velocity, comparative combat dynamics and high-calibre machine-gun rounds per minute. We paused momentarily, heads bowed, in front of a MiG-3 with the legend *Za Rodinu* (For the Motherland) written in Cyrillic on the fuselage—a plane that her uncle, also an engineer, had worked on during World War II. 'Not so effective at low altitude,' she said after a while, and I wondered if this statement was also true of Natasha herself, reduced now to the role of administrator rather than serving the greater glory of the revolution.

Later that evening, as if to compete with Natasha's tour, we visited Zulfyia's grandparents in their flat overlooking the Kazanka River. Her Tatar grandfather, also a military engineer and proud defender of the Soviet Union, brought out a bottle of toxic blood-coloured *samagon* (his own cherry-flavoured home-brewed vodka). The label showed him with a vast chestful of Soviet military medals from long years of service and glorious campaigns putting down nascent liberation movements—Budapest '56 and Prague '68. At 94 per cent proof, the lethal liquid had not only fuelled the troops under his command but probably the aircraft as well. To shouts of '*Allahu al-Akhbar!*' (God is Great) we drank shots of the stuff until my weak Western constitution could take no more and I collapsed in bed.

Kazan is an ancient city, founded by Turkic-speaking Tatars as part of the great Mongol Empire—the Golden Horde—that stretched through Siberia, Russia, Central Asia, China and the Middle East a thousand years ago. The empire had run as a federation of subordinate tribute-paying khanates of which Kazan, located in central Russia on the banks of the Volga River, was an important trading centre. Kazan was also one of the first to fall to the rising power of medieval Moscow and its claims to the mantle of the Roman Empire after the fall of Byzantium.

Modern Kazan reflected these influences and had become, in the post-1989 world, a curiosity inside the Russian Federation. It is the most northern of Muslim cities, located at the centre of Russia rather than the troubled post-imperial periphery, and links road, rail, air and river trade routes. It is close enough to the Ural Mountains to boast that it is the 'Gateway to Siberia' but is also an integral part of the 'European' Russia. Kazan was at once key to post-Soviet Russian unity and yet also symbolic of Russia's ongoing negotiation of its place between Europe and Asia.

'I am in Asia,' Catherine the Great had written to Voltaire on entering Kazan in 1767. 'In Kazan, there are twenty different peoples which are nothing like each other and I have to sew, for them, one garment to suit everyone'. Similarly, the philosopher and revolutionary Alexander Herzen observed that the 'significance of Kazan is very great: it is a place where two worlds meet. So it has two beginnings: Western and Eastern, and you can see them at every crossroads; here they lived together and became friendly as a result of the unending interaction, and here they began to produce something quite original of their own'.

With a population equally comprised of ethnic Russians and nominally Muslim, Turkic-speaking Tatars (as well as small Jewish and Volga German populations) Tatarstan was in many ways everything that the Muslim experience of the end of the Soviet Union was not. This was no Chechnya, Abkhazia, Ossetia or Dagestan; the notorious and vicious Caucasian conflicts. Instead it was stable, had relative wealth (through oil and natural gas), and with more than a million people Kazan was a major urban centre. Tatarstan was an Autonomous Republic within the Russian Federation and its then president, Mintimer Shaimiev, had effortlessly made the transition from Communist Party chief to president with all the democratic legitimacy and symbolism that a repainted Kremlin office could confer. For this, he was lauded by the United States, visited by George Bush Senior, Bill Clinton, German chancellor Gerhardt Schröder and financial luminaries including George Soros.

Kazan even featured in an article in the *Atlantic Monthly* in which the journalist, after a short stroll through Kazan's one and only shopping strip, declared it to be a triumph of capitalism. The mass poverty hidden away in drab suburban tower blocks, the grindingly low wages, the alcoholism, the declining life spans, the barter economy and the ubiquitous presence of maimed Afghan war veterans without pride or pension begging on the side of the road were mere details to the triumph of the market. At least now you could get a decently tailored suit in Bauman Street, something that had been unheard of since 1917, and vote for the republic's politicians as long as you didn't choose anyone not already in office.

Revolutions, it has been said, have a tendency to devour their children and this was especially true of Russia in the 1990s. From what I could see, Kazan had become, like much of the rest of Russia, a 'babushka economy'. The disappearance of the old order had knocked the perestroika generation sideways. 'We used to have a beautiful ideal,' one of my students told me. He had been a young Soviet army officer, highly trained in electronic engineering at the time of the collapse, and had made a successful transition to the private sector as a pioneer of the new middle class. 'But now we sell cigarettes.' Young, educated and adaptable, he made the transition well, but for the overwhelming majority it had been a catastrophe eliminating employment in 'unproductive' industries, and most forms of state social investment from schools to roads, farms, hospitals and pensions. The middle generation, brought up under the old regime but not yet familiar with the new one, or insufficiently well-connected with it, failed to cope and died off at levels higher than the birth rate—lost to alcoholic oblivion and drug-induced despair. Average life expectancy had declined by over a decade since the collapse of the Soviet Union. As a consequence, families were propped up not by the young and the economically active but by the grandmothers, widows of the earlier lost generation of World War II (which claimed in excess of 23 million Soviet lives)—the 'babushkas'. In an irony that would only become clear to me years later, these widows often spoke some basic German, limited as my landlady once told me to the contradictory imperatives of the invading army: 'Hands up!' and 'Help me!' These were exactly the same phrases, learned this time in Russian, that were repeated to me by Afghan refugees who had lived through the Soviet invasion of Afghanistan and had fled subsequent conflict sixty years later.

The babushkas were everywhere—running the market stalls, selling clothes, producing unappetising mounds of turnip and beetroot, and making deliciously warm hand-knitted socks and gloves for winter. They scoured the streets and shops for deals, looked after children, and ran homes. One morning, as I was returning from an evening out—the perpetual night of the Russian winter easing slightly into a grey dawn, little lighter than the static of a dead television station—I encountered a group of people standing on the street corner. As I approached, I saw that they were all elderly babushkas, heavy steel icepicks in hand, cracking the black ice from the pavements in temperatures approaching minus 30 degrees so that the morning's passers-by could walk the pavements and shop in safety.

The black ice was so treacherous that every so often I would find myself flying unexpectedly through the air to land with a painful crack, flat on my back. I even took to sliding my way home from work sitting on my briefcase—large enough to act as a kind of sled—and, despite the treacherous conditions, sliding fast down the pavements as dusk approached soon became, along with learning to ice-skate, one of the daily pleasures of living in Kazan in the winter.

I discussed this with my Russian friends. 'You must stride less,' they said. 'Keep your feet on the ground—you must learn to "walk like a babushka".' Despite plaudits from the great and the good of the West, vast oil and natural gas wealth, and the capital of Moscow with the highest number of millionaires per capita in the world, for Tatarstan, and much of the rest of Russia, the babushka-centric daily economy seemed to indicate that it was a country going in reverse. While the arms race and the prospect of mutually assured nuclear destruction during the Cold War had failed to bring down the communist bloc, joked British comedian Rory Bremner, introduce capitalism and 'they're screwed for a generation'.

'Let's start with the most important word in any language,' said Arthur from deep inside a gothic pseudo-German beer hall called Bar Grot—'cigarette'. I'd undertaken to learn Russian and was starting informally by exchanging Russian lessons for chess with a young Oxford exchange student at Kazan State University. Arthur was brilliant and chess was possibly the only field of knowledge where I held a brief and rapidly diminishing advantage. I had been stunned when I encountered him in the university corridors, not having heard another native English speaker for over three months. First came the voice—slow, resonant and authoritative—followed by the apparition of someone who resembled a young Rumpole, shuffling with babushka-like mastery of the conditions through the university.

It was a great university closely linked with Russia's cultural and political past—Tolstoy had failed his final exams there, Lenin had been expelled after organising a demonstration against the regime in his first week, and Gorky had failed the entrance exam. With my mediocre attempts to master Russian in exchange for chess, I was privileged to be in such company. 'In fifty years' time,' Arthur claimed, 'people will wish they could say they had been, not in Oxford or Berkeley or the Sorbonne, but in Kazan.' And we embarked on the search for the 'cultural vortex'—to find that point between East and West that Herzen had identified as unique to the Tatar lands.

I sought this initially among my colleagues at the language school. When I started, there were no students and I was the only teacher, and I tried to satisfy my curiosity through idiosyncratic recruiting. At first I thought a retired Tatar schoolteacher would be my guide to the inner workings of the city. He appeared one day at the office in response to an ad—a small and hawk-like man with sharp, twinkling eyes that I almost imagined were on the lookout for prey. He had spent his entire working life in Kazan's schools and offered to teach me Tatar. But on the appointed day he failed to show up, and never responded to phone calls—later we found out that he had died shortly after our job offer.

Another teacher I thought would be interesting was Zemfira, an elderly Kazakh woman who had also spent her working life teaching in Kazan's schools. Zulya was sceptical—too old-fashioned, too formal and 'Soviet' in her approach—and referred to her in private as 'Kazakh Woman'. But I found her fascinating, and in addition to early conversations about life in Soviet Kazakhstan and about her visit to the Baikonur Cosmodrome (the USSR's space launching site) on an excursion from the collective farm where she worked, she had the most amazing set of silver false teeth I had ever seen. Once a status symbol in the Soviet Union, silver teeth had become an undesirable relic in the fashionable New Russia with its conspicuous advertisements and image consciousness. Advertisers had even begun to import models from Holland who had the desired 'Western look' rather than risk being associated with the grey drabness of the Soviet past somehow deemed manifest in the Russian physiognomy.

Unfortunately, in the classroom she was a total disaster. Students loathed her 'Soviet' methods—all lectures, dictation and rote learning—and they complained so much that she eventually left. I had not found the 'vortex' but I did learn never to recruit someone solely on the basis of dentistry.

Being one of the very few 'Westerners' in Kazan and certainly the only Australian, I inadvertently became a very minor celebrity. While dozing off during the fifth act of Mussorgsky's opera *Boris Godunov* at the Kazan Opera House, a vast neo-classical building built in the 1950s by German prisoners of war, I was elbowed in the ribs by a young woman sitting in the row behind. As I embarked on an apology, fearing that I'd fatally cast aspersions on one of the great works of Russian civilisation, she whispered loudly, 'Do you like tennis?' Despite my better instincts, and still on the increasingly quixotic pursuit of the vortex, I said yes. At the end of the act she issued me with instructions to meet her the next day at a location near the university.

Wondering where we would play tennis in the middle of the Russian winter, I set off and soon found myself not in some ice-bound tennis court, but in a small and grotty recording studio with a translator.

'Thank God you've arrived,' said my mysterious operatic assailant from the previous evening. 'I have to present a tennis program on the radio today, but I don't know anything about tennis.'

I turned, ashen-faced, to the translator, who had inter-jected by saying that he detested all sport particularly tennis, and felt obliged to confess that I didn't know anything about tennis either. But it was too late—we were on air and I discovered that I was on Kazan's niche talkback tennis show.

Feeling like a player without a racket bracing himself for the first serve before an imagined audience of millions, the first question was 'Have you ever seen a kangaroo?' After that the barrage was fierce and relentless: 'How many rubles is tennis in Australia?', 'Can you name the most famous tennis player in Tatarstan?' and, increasingly unimpressed with my answers, one aggravated listener asked, 'Do you know anything about any other sport?'

I sang the praises of Russian tennis, lauded the great contribution of Kazan to the sport over the centuries and hoped that the translator, who by now had assumed an atti-tude of superior boredom and contempt, was making it all sound better in Russian.

As I left the studio still racking my brain for any tennis-related trivia I could think of, a large black sedan screeched to a stop on the kerb next to me. A woman dressed in pink threw open the door and said in tones that presented no alternative, 'Ivan wants to see you.' So I got in and was driven at speed to the headquarters of Kanal 6, Kazan's main commercial TV network. Ivan turned out to be the head of news and, like the tennis presenter, had found himself in a sporting quandary: it was the opening ceremony of the Sydney Olympics and he, too, needed to find something to say. And so I was placed in front of a very small TV screen in the basement of Kanal 6 trying desperately to work out what to say about the Olympic Games. The figures on the screen were distant and tiny and the parade of Australiana was even more absurd when viewed from a place that styled itself as the Gateway to Siberia.

Mounted cattlemen charged to the theme of *The Man from Snowy River*, boys and girls moved like ants with what appeared to be corrugated-iron sheets and water tanks, a horde of people seemed to be mowing a giant lawn, while an enormous octopus turned red and slowly floated into the night sky. In a moment of desperate genius, Ivan came up with something to say—'What is your favourite Olympic sport?' he asked. I seized the moment and said how much I looked forward to some strong competition in the synchronised swimming. That night as I watched the news I saw myself on screen, dubbed into a deep basso profundo Russian, apparently sounding very knowledgeable about the Tatar athletes competing at the games, the origins of the Olympics and how proud I was to see Sydney on the world stage. It really didn't matter what I said—Ivan had got his Australian, and my pursuit of the cultural vortex had produced bizarre results.

Zulya summoned me to the office one day. 'You must do something. A man called Adam has been here every day asking for you. We don't know what he wants, he just comes and sits and asks to speak to you. Please talk to him for us,' she implored, clearly sick of this stranger occupying her days.

Adam was an exceptionally tall Sudanese, of South Sudan's Dinka ethnicity. He had come to Kazan on a scholarship from the then Soviet-allied Khartoum and had studied engineering. His achievements were spectacular—not only had he learned Russian fluently (as well as speaking Dinka, English and Arabic) but from war-torn Sudan, where few had primary schooling, he had gone on to earn a doctorate in a country known for the incredible rigor of its scientific education. He was now a research assistant at the Kazan's specialist institute for designing power plants. But there it had stopped. War had prevented his return to Sudan, and the collapse of the Soviet Union had eroded his pay to a pittance and led him to rely on part-time and marginal jobs at the institute. He wore thin shoes against waist-height snow and ice, and could not afford a new coat even though his was now threadbare. He was now getting by on $20 a month—his salary from the institute—and in the university canteen I asked him what he ate. 'Only potatoes,' he said woefully.

Adam could not return to Sudan and we discussed migration to Britain or Australia—both of which he had tried and failed. I suggested teaching at Linguamir, at least for extra cash, but this would jeopardise his proper work at the power plant and was not feasible. Or so he said, but underlying this was the knowledge that as an African he would never fit in, even in as diverse a place as Kazan. Racism was on the rise in Russia: leather-jacketed skinhead gangs (called Gopniks) were on the streets and an English friend had recently been beaten up when gang members heard his accented Russian. The graffiti at the local cinema said (in English) 'Fuck Nigger' and there was an increasingly disturbing ultra-nationalism which meant that, beyond the liberal institute where he worked and where he was valued for his abilities, Adam would never be accepted, let alone employed. In any case, even if he earned $50 a month instead, this was not going to change things substantially. His one remaining option, he said, was the Mormons, who had recently been allowed into Russia and had set up a meeting hall in a former chess school.

We met a number of times—going to the canteen where I would buy him lunch or dinner and ensure that there wasn't a potato to be seen. But increasingly he spent his time with the missionaries of the Latter Day Saints, knowing that this might be his last, if severely circumscribed, chance of a future outside Russia. As we parted company, he cut a forbidding picture of isolation walking off down Bauman Street, past its designer shops, a lone African student in the Russian winter left behind by the consequences of state collapse. In an apocalyptic sudden reversion back to the Middle Ages, this highly trained scientist was now forced to seek a future in the ideological obscurantism of the Mormon church.

Late one night after an evening at Bar Grot, our small party walked out into the deepest cold of the winter. It was minus 30, a fresh snow had fallen while we were inside and the crystalline night was still, hard and clear. Arthur's beard turned instantly white with frost and we stood collectively awed by this perfect ice world. On a hill above us, a fort that predated Moscow's conquest of the Tatar lands—the Kremlin—stood white and illuminated against the night sky. Inside we could see twin cathedrals: the onion domes of the Orthodox Church, like alien planets hovering just above the city, and a reconstructed Tatar mosque whose minaret soared into the firmament.

'Let's storm the Kremlin,' someone shouted and we ran, ploughing through the snow, straight at the hill and the tall crenellated walls. On we went, even as the snow reached waist height, swimming almost through the crisp powder, falling, picking ourselves up and lurching onwards to the spire and the domes. Snow got into my boots and down the back of my neck as I plunged headfirst into the embankment, an exhilarating razor-shock of cold that set my senses on edge. I crashed on, into the steepest part of the ascent, inhaling stabbing Arctic breath and covered in a thick white down of snow. In a final staggering lunge, I fell against the summit and reached out to touch the base of the walls with my bare hands. And lying there I looked up, beyond the blur of white, past the vertiginous Kremlin defences and deep into the night. Over Freedom Square, the new Russian tricolour fluttered and I could just make out the statue of Lenin striding forth in bronze perpetuity in the direction of the Opera House and the up-market shops on Bauman Street, and in the distance came the muffled Tatar-accented humming of the morning's call to prayer.

EPILOGUE

Rich Arabic coffee served in the desert. The Himalayan night sky. An evening walk through a camp as families talk and prepare meals. Such ordinary moments of reflection and reprieve forge bonds with people and place in extreme contexts such as state collapse, natural disaster and conflict. If the majority of the stories in this book occur in countries and societies at the point of crisis, they are also about connection and disconnection—negotiating the new and immediate cultural, political and institutional demands of humanitarian work. This is work that often jarringly sets worlds and realities in contrast to each other in ways that illuminate and question. And despite the problems of humanitarian assistance—who should do it, how it should be done, and how effective it may be—it is this sense of curiosity and the desire to think and explore, while also performing a function during the day's work, that is the source of humanitarian action and, ultimately, of the view that things can and should be different. Much of this comes down to dollars and cents—vital funds that allow institutions to act and to engage—but it is also much more than that. It is about learning to live with complexity and somehow negotiating a path through, no matter how arduous, that does not see lives as numbers, or 'stories' that fit a media cycle, or the deliberately heart-rending advertisements of an aid agency.

In the context of Australian and European angst over asylum seekers—especially those arriving by boat—it is precisely this inability to see a fuller, more complex humanitarian picture, a lack of appreciation perhaps for the concept of humanity itself, that leads to a continuation of suffering. Ironically, it is often the spirit of generosity and enquiry that is most evident in the societies whose people are on the receiving end of natural disasters, conflict, or at the forefront of climate change. If anything, this is what humanitarians can bring back to their homes and their own societies—an answer, perhaps, to Bertold Brecht's stark poem about humanitarian assistance, in which a man at the corner of 26th Street and Broadway in New York, collects money to provide beds for the homeless.

It won't change the world
It won't improve relations among men
It will not shorten the age of exploitation
But a few men have a bed for the night
For a night the wind is kept from them
The snow meant for them falls on the roadway.

ACKNOWLEDGEMENTS

I would like to thank Eamon Evans for being an early guide to the publishing industry and Rose Michael at Hardie Grant for her patience, encouragement, and willingness to take a chance. Penelope Goodes has been a talented editor and helped turn what risked becoming an essay into a book. Special thanks are due to the staff of the Swinburne Institute for Social Research for their ongoing support and for being a sounding-board for much of the material in this book.

Parts of the Pakistan section appeared in *Griffith Review* 35 'Surviving' as 'How to Survive an Earthquake'; parts of the Sudan chapter appeared in *Granta* 117 'Horror' as 'The Mission' and in *Gesher* 2012 as 'Homage to Darfur'.